感染拡大

.hack Part 1
DOT

INFECTION

OFFICIAL STRATEGY GUIDE

BY DOUG WALSH

TABLE OF CONTENTS

INTRO

The year is 2010 and a young boy named Kite has finally obtained a copy of "The World," the best-selling massively multiplayer online role playing game (MMORPG) that his friends have been raving about for months. The time has finally come for Kite to create his user profile and join one of his friends online. That friend, Orca, has promised to take the newbie under his wing and show him the ins and outs of online gaming. Unfortunately, Kite's friend Orca, known in "The World" as Orca of the Azure Sky, encounters an abnormally difficult creature in one of the beginner's dungeons. This never-before-seen monster strikes down Orca with such ferocity that he is wiped clear from the game environment. Weirder still is the fact that Orca's real-life persona is knocked into a coma as a result of the battle.

Shortly after Kite learns of the horrible news concerning Orca, he receives a mystical bracelet that possesses the ability to weed out infected monsters in "The World" and drain them of their virus-ridden data files. To learn more of his friend's condition, Kite must rely on the people he meets online and the information he can gather from messages posted on the Board, the official bulletin board for "The World." Throughout the course of his adventure, Kite will make numerous friends who are all too willing to help him in his quest. In fact, some are a little *too* helpful and may not be trusted.

Although *.hack//INFECTION* is strictly an offline single-player RPG, the developers have created a game within a game that not only imitates the complexity of an epic MMORPG, but has succeeded in creating two distinct worlds. In assuming the role of Kite, the player must navigate both the real world and the one fabricated by the CC Corporation. Kite must learn to build relationships with other players, both inside "The World" and through email in reality. He must navigate the numerous postings on message boards and learn how to properly communicate and trade with strangers in the game environment. Yes, in taking the role of Kite, the player must master what should be a familiar role, that of a gamer. Of course, the stakes have never been higher: conquer "The World" to save a friend's life and expose the evildoings of a maverick game publishing company.

A SERIES OF FOUR

.hack//INFECTION is the first volume in a four-part series of games. Keep this fact in mind when playing through the game, as several items may not be usable until later installments of the game. Also, the player will gain access to lists of enemies, players, and grunties that contain placeholders for future installments. It's very important to save your game progress after completing this volume of the game, as completed game data is compatible with future installments in the series. In fact, even after completing *.hack//INFECTION* the player can continue to battle in the dungeons to "level up" in preparation for the next volume.

GETTING STARTED

Playing *.hack//INFECTION* is akin to playing two games at once, as the story centers around a young boy's experience with an online role-playing game called "The World." In addition to controlling the boy's decisions while he sits in front of his computer in the real world, players also assume the role of his player-character in the virtual arena. Although the transition from the world that is real to that which is fantasy is a smooth one, players must take a moment to set up their "account" before getting started. The player's suspension of disbelief will go uninterrupted once these minor tasks are completed.

Game Options

- **Controller:** Select one of the four pre-configured controller setups. Although the face buttons won't change, the movement and camera controls can be mapped to other buttons.

- **Vibrate:** Toggle the controller's vibration functions on/off.

- **Adjust Screen:** Use the D-Pad to adjust horizontal (X) and vertical (Y) position of the screen.

- **Sound:** Use the sliders to adjust the level of the Main Volume, the Background Music (BGM), and the Sound Effects (SE). Select between mono and stereo outputs.

- **Voiceover:** Choose between English and Japanese for verbal dialogue.

- **Movie Text:** Toggle dialog boxes on/off.

New Game

After the introduction, you have the opportunity to create a User Name and Character Name. Enter any name you'd like for the User Name and select Enter. Although the Character Name can be changed as well, the default name "Kite" is used throughout this book. Confirm the two name choices on the following screen to complete the registration process.

ONE AND THE SAME

To prevent confusion, the name Kite is always used to refer to your character in the game, both inside and outside of "The World." Although this young boy does have a real name, as do the other players he encounters, they only use their online identities—even when emailing one another.

THE DESKTOP

Now that "The World" has been successfully installed and Kite is registered on the network, it's time to get familiar with the desktop. The desktop is essentially Kite's computer monitor, where he can access the game, email, get news updates, and add to his ever-growing collection of multimedia. This following section covers each option that appears on the desktop.

- **"The World":** Select this icon to logon to "The World." When the game commences, the player can read messages posted on the game-specific BBS (Bulletin Board System) or enter the game world via the server on which he last played.

Mailer: This is Kite's email program, which is used to communicate with other players outside the game environment. Although Kite cannot initiate conversation through email, he can reply to many of the emails that he receives. These emails reveal important information that can help Kite progress through "The World," and help increase the affection other players feel toward him. A notification appears when Kite receives new email in his inbox.

News: Don't get too immersed while playing "The World," or you'll miss out on all of the current events unfolding around the planet. Check this news-viewing program to find out all the latest about the Altimit Corporation and other hot topics of the day.

Accessory: This option enables the user to change the image that appears on the desktop. Although there are only three options when the game begins (Orange Blossom, Red Eye, and Blue Moon), dozens of images are unlocked throughout the course of the game.

Audio: The Altimit operating system (OS) comes equipped with one selection of background music (BGM), but many more are unlocked by playing "The World." Additionally, the player can unlock movies to watch. Unlike the images and songs, you must complete *.hack//INFECTION* to view them.

Data: This option enables the user to save his/her game progress while not logged into "The World."

Before logging into "The World," check the email and read the news updates. Kite has three emails in his inbox: two from CC Corporation regarding "The World" and one from Yasuhiko, his friend who is waiting to show him the ins and outs of playing online. Read each email for pertinent information about the newest version of the game (version 2.75), plus details on moving between the various servers. Inspect the news to keep on top of what's hot, then logon to "The World."

"THE WORLD" TITLE SCREEN

Yasuhiko is waiting in Root Town, but Kite will become less of a newbie when he gets there if he first reads some of the messages on the Board. The Board is a place where many of the players gather to share information about strategies and locations they've explored. Much of the information included in these early threads is described in greater detail in the "Advanced Hacking" chapter. When finished, select Log In from the title screen to access "The World."

Thread: Zeit Statue   **Author: Admin of Time**

The Zeit Statue at the bottom of the dungeon is searching for an adventurer to give a title of honor as the "Hero of Zeit."

Only way to get the title is to get to the Zeit Statue as fast as you can!

Those who want the praise of the Zeit Statue select Chronicling as your part A at the Chaos Gate.

*First look for an area with a dungeon close to the entrance that doesn't have that many floors. The Hero of Zeit must also be versed in looking for an advantageous area.

Orca's Tutorial

Kite's friend is patiently waiting by the Chaos Gate in the Δ Server's Root Town. This being his first time playing an online role-playing game, Kite is unfamiliar with certain aspects of the gaming culture, specifically the use of screen names instead of real names. Orca quickly counsels Kite on his miscue and offers him his member address. Now Kite can send Orca a Flash Mail invitation to join his party.

Follow Orca's instructions by pressing the △ button and selecting Party from the Personal Menu Screen. Select the name of a person you'd like to join your party and press the ✕ button to confirm it. Only those players who give out their member addresses can be invited.

With Orca in the party, approach the Chaos Gate and press the ✕ button to access the menu screen. Select New Keyword from the list. Follow Orca's recommendation and input the keywords Bursting, Passed Over, and Aqua Field for Part A, Part B, and Part C, respectively. This combination yields an area with a Battle Level 1, which is perfect for beginners. Select Warp from the list to enter the first battle area.

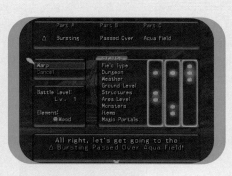

FLASH MAIL

As Orca points out, Flash Mail is accessible only while Kite is in one of the server's towns. Also, since Flash Mail only works in "The World," those people not currently logged in to the game won't have the ability to reply. However, players who are logged in will almost always transfer to the town Kite is in after being mailed. Use this function to amass a party of three characters (including Kite) before preparing to head into battle.

 Δ: BURSTING, PASSED OVER, AQUA FIELD

RECOMMENDED PARTY: KITE AND ORCA

AREA VITALS		MONSTERS	ITEMS		GOTT STATUE ITEMS
BATTLE LEVEL:	1	FIELD:	Resurrect	The Hanged Man	Steel Blades
ELEMENT:	Wood	Goblin: Earth	Gale Breath	Healing Potion	Yellow Candy
GRUNTY FOOD:	Mandragora	DUNGEON:	Speed Charm		Grunt Doll
ENVIRONMENT:	Grassland	Goblin: Earth			
WEATHER:	Partly Cloudy	Magical Goblin: Fire			
		Disco Knife			

Orca is an expert at instructing new players in the ways of "The World." He will methodically teach Kite all he needs to know about controlling the camera and engaging while in combat. The table on the next page details the default controller settings.

CONTROLS

BUTTON	WHAT IT DOES
✕ button	Attack/Confirm selection
◯ button	Cancel
▢ button	Chat Commands
△ button	Personal Menu
L1 button	Rotate camera left
R1 button	Rotate camera right
L2 button	Switch between first- and third-person perspectives
R2 button	Center camera behind Kite
Left Analog Stick	Movement
Right Analog Stick	Rotate camera and zoom in and out
Directional Pad	Movement
Select button	Hide/Show area map
Start button	Pause Menu

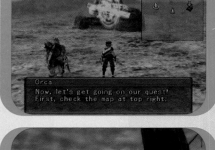

After explaining the camera system, Orca explains the difference between the field and the dungeon. When entering a new area, the party always first appears on the field, or the aboveground landscape. Although the group is free to enter the dungeon immediately, it's best to thoroughly search the field first to help the group level up quicker. In addition, there are other items and places in the field that will prove beneficial to Kite. These items are described later.

Orca uses a Fairy's Orb to display the unknown areas on the map. This item enables the group to see each of the Magic Portals on the map in the upper right-hand corner of the screen. Each Magic Portal contains monsters and/or treasure chests. Although they have no further significance in the field, many Magic Portals in the dungeons are connected to the various doors and gates in the underground rooms. The party will oftentimes need to kill the monster or open the treasure chest to break the spell and gain access to adjacent rooms.

Rush straight ahead toward one of the Magic Portals. Follow Orca's advice and repeatedly slash at the Goblin that spawns by pressing the ✕ button—don't worry, it won't fight back! Kite earns 60 EXP for defeating the lowly Goblin!

Orca's next lesson is about Skills. Follow his instructions on accessing the Personal Menu, then select Skills. Once in the Skills Menu, use the D-Pad or the R1 Button to flip to the Recovery page and select the Repth skill. There are many different skills to acquire, but it's important to note that skills can't be purchased or traded for individually. Skills are just one of the many attributes that comprise armor and weaponry; they can't be separated from those items. This means that when a player equips a different type of weapon, the skills associated with the previous weapon are no longer usable.

SKILLS MENU

SKILL	DECRIPTION
Attack	Weapons-based attacks that must be performed at close range.
Magic	Spell-based attacks that can be performed from a distance.
Recovery	Spells that heal and revive party members.
Strengthen	Spells that buff party members' attributes.
Weaken	Spells used to decrease enemy attributes.
Data Drain	Special attack used by Kite. See the "Advanced Hacking" chapter for more information.

With an elementary understanding of Skills and combat, it's time for Orca to teach Kite about Chat Commands. Press the ⬚ button to access the Chat Commands Menu screen. This is how you provide commands to your allies. Orca instructs Kite on issuing the First Aid! command. This command tells the other party members to concentrate their efforts on using recovery skills that will heal and cure allies in need of assistance. Chat Commands are an important piece of the overall strategy that must be employed to succeed in "The World."

There are three main types of Chat Commands. You can specify a particular *Skill Usage*, an overall *Strategy*, or select an individual *Member* and give him/her specific commands. Each type of Chat Command is described in the following tables.

DO AS I SAY, NOT AS I DO

One of the benefits of being the party leader is that you can tell the party members to do whatever you'd like while you concentrate on something else. For example, it's perfectly acceptable to order your allies to concentrate on performing healing while you attack the enemy. In other words, the Chat Commands do *not* govern your own personal attack strategy, only that of your allies.

SKILL USAGE COMMANDS

SKILL	DESCRIPTION
Skills!	All party members use physical and magical attack skills and items instead of traditional combat.
First Aid!	Party members concentrate on using recovery skills and items to keep the party healthy.
Weaken!	Orders party members to use weakening skills and items against enemies.
Strengthen!	Orders party members to use strengthening skills and items on allies.
Don't Use Skills!	Allies attack with their weapons in melee-style combat. This is an excellent way to dispose of lesser enemies.
Attack!	Orders allies to use physical attack skills. This command is not recommended when the party contains a Wavemaster.
Magic!	Orders allies to use magical attack skills and items in battle. This is a great way to ensure that your party members don't stray too close to a powerful foe.

STRATEGY COMMANDS

STRATEGY	DESCRIPTION
Operation Wonder Battle	The default strategy. It orders allies to attack the closest enemy to them without using skills or items.
Operation Union Battle	The entire party gangs up on whatever enemy Kite attacks. This is great for times when one large enemy is accompanied by lesser foes that can be ignored.
Operation Follow Me	The party travels together in a close formation and only engages in battle if attacked at close range.
Operation Recover	Orders allies to not move and instead concentrate on recovering themselves.

MEMBER COMMANDS

COMMAND	DESCRIPTION
Designate Skill	Select a specific skill to be used by a party member. This choice grants the player access to an ally's Skills Menu.
Change Equipment	Access an ally's equipment screens and make changes to his or her equipped weapons and armor. This is especially useful when entering an area with a different element than the previous one.
First Aid!	Order a specific ally to use recovery skills and items, thereby leaving the other party members free to continue attacking.
Designate Target	Select a specific enemy for an ally to target. This is an excellent way to ensure a Wavemaster attacks an enemy that has Physical Tolerance.
Assemble	Orders an ally to stick close to Kite and only attack enemies if they are close by. This is recommended if an ally's battle level is less than that of the area monsters.
Standby	Orders a party member to stand ground and recover himself.

GUIDING PRINCIPALS

The Chat Commands listed in the Strategy menu represent general strategies that the party will follow for extended periods of time. Although the majority of these strategies forbid the use of skills, you can use the Skills Usage and Member commands to override the general strategy for a specific battle. The attack pattern (Wonder Battle, Union, or Follow Me) will still be followed.

A Little Time to Think

One of the game's great features is that time automatically stands still whenever the Chat Commands screen or Personal Menu screen is accessed. This means that the player can access either screen to pause the battle and carefully assess the situation, then dole out the most effective commands for any situation. Consider using the Designate Target function to investigate the element, tolerances, and current HP of nearby enemies. You can exit all menu screens without making a selection by pressing the ◯ button.

Finish off the Goblins in each of the three other Magic Portals on the field, then head toward the red arrow on the map and venture down into the dungeon. Things will get a bit tougher in the dungeon, so don't forget anything you just learned!

Dungeon, B1

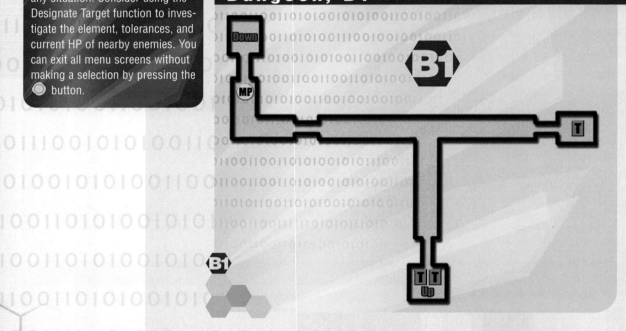

There are a couple of chests in the dungeon's entrance room. The yellow chest is known as a Treasure. To open it, target it and press the ✕ button. The blue chest, on the other hand, is known as a Risky Treasure. To safely open it, you need a *Fortune Wire*. A Fortune Wire disarms the trap, thus making the chest safe to open. Although Kite can normally withstand the damage or curse inflicted by opening a Risky Treasure without a Fortune Wire, the valuable item inside will go unseen!

After going through the doorway to the next room, Kite and Orca catch a glimpse of an angelic girl fleeing from an enormous creature carrying a red cross. Orca knows that a creature that powerful shouldn't be on this level. Head down the hall and turn to the right at the T intersection to inspect the room where the girl fled. Unfortunately, the girl and the monster have disappeared. Open the Treasure and head off in the other direction down the corridor.

The doors leading in and out of the next room slam shut behind the party. To open them, all of the Magic Portals in the room must be activated. Kill the Goblin that emerges from the portal and continue down the stairs in the next room to the lower level of the dungeon.

Dungeon, B2

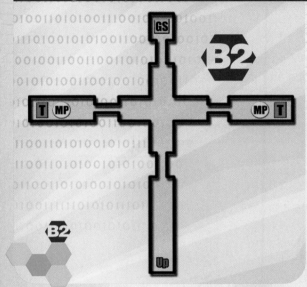

This dungeon has two very small floors. Continue toward the intersection and explore the rooms off to the right and left. Each room contains a Magic Portal and a pair of enemies. Make sure you explore both rooms before moving straight ahead, because this enables Kite to clear all of the dungeon portals. Successfully clearing all of the Magic Portals in a dungeon is just one of the many statistics that will eventually help the player unlock a multitude of secrets.

Enter the room north of the intersection to find the Gott Statue. One of these statues is located at the deepest level in every dungeon; it's there to serve as a reward to the hearty adventurers who find them. Unlike the Treasures that litter the dungeon and field, the one at the Gott Statue contains three valuable items, including a weapon or armor.

Ironically, Orca mentions to Kite that they are without a Spirit Ocarina so they must trudge back through the dungeon to the stairs leading up to the field. Upon exiting the Gott Statue room, they are swept away to a faraway location within "The World." The little girl they saw being chased approaches Orca and hands him a mysterious book before disappearing into thin air. Moments later, the creature that was chasing the girl arrives on the scene and unleashes an unthinkable attack against Orca. Then, just as the creature begins to fix his sights on Kite, a mighty staff is thrust into the ground between the two and the game crashes. Despite the system error, the book that was meant for Orca is passed on to Kite as his character lies on the ground motionless.

Kite eventually logs out of "The World" and frantically calls Orca on the phone to see if he's okay. Unfortunately, Kite learns that Orca has been hospitalized and is in a coma. Could it be because of what happened online? Either way, Kite has plenty of time to figure out his next move. Use the Data option on the desktop to save your game and read the next chapter to learn the many "Advanced Hacking" techniques that will better prepare you for the adventures to come.

ADVANCED HACKING

It's important to understand the fundamentals of playing RPGs, like managing an inventory, acquiring EXP, and leveling up. Additionally, there are many gameplay elements specific to "The World," such as trading with other PCs, interacting with the Spring of Myst, and using the Data Drain and Gate Hacking powers of the bracelet.

RPG BASICS

RPGs require the player to assume the role of a character who must focus on growing stronger and solving an intricate story. In addition, the character must manage a large inventory of weapons and items, master dozens of magical skills, and interact with numerous characters in the game environment.

Experience

Experience (EXP) is gained whenever the party members defeat an enemy in battle. The exact number of EXP allotted is based on the level of the enemy relative to Kite's level. Winning a battle against an equal or stronger enemy yields a larger amount of EXP than defeating a much weaker foe. Better yet, each member is awarded a full amount of EXP as if he/she had won the battle single-handedly. The EXP awarded depends on how far apart his or her level is from the defeated monster.

Gaining EXP is important for several reasons. For starters, the player's level increases per 1000 EXP earned. This is referred to as "leveling up." A higher level means the player is becoming stronger and possesses higher attack and defense ratings. Even more important is the fact that the character's maximum capacity of Hit Points (HP) and Skill Points (SP) increases as well. More HP enables the character to survive more potent attacks, while having more SP permits the use of more powerful skills.

EXP DISTRIBUTION BASED ON MONSTER'S LEVEL RELATIVE TO PLAYER'S LEVEL	
DIFF. IN LEVEL	EXP AWARDED
-10	1
-9	2
-8	3
-7	4
-6	6
-5	8
-4	13
-3	28
-2	40
-1	50
0	60
1	70
2	80
3	100
4	130
5	170
6	220
7	280
8	350
9	430
10	520

Elements

Many of the enemies in "The World" are aligned with one of six elements: Earth, Wood, Water, Fire, Thunder, or Darkness. Those possessing a particular elemental alignment can withstand attacks by that element. For example, a Fire Witch isn't harmed as severely by a Fire-based magic scroll as a creature not aligned with Fire.

It's possible to put an enemy's elemental alignment to use against it. Each element has an opposing element as detailed in the following table. In keeping with the Fire Witch example, by using a Water-based skill against it, there's a very good chance that an "Elemental Hit" will take place. Elemental Hits are particularly deadly attacks and deliver much more damage than normal attacks. It's important to try to counter each monster's alignment with an Elemental Hit, especially when fighting creatures with lots of HP.

Color	Element	Opposing Element
Orange	Earth	Wood
Green	Wood	Earth
Red	Fire	Water
Blue	Water	Fire
Yellow	Thunder	Darkness
Purple	Darkness	Thunder

Some enemies aren't only aligned with an element, but have a tolerance instead. A creature with a particular elemental tolerance can't be harmed by an attack aligned with that element. For example, a creature with a Thunder Tolerance will receive no damage from a Thunder-based attack. Items known as Banes remove an enemy's tolerance, but it's often easier to attack with a skill linked to the opposing element.

OTHER TOLERANCES

In addition to elemental tolerances, some creatures possess a Physical or Magical Tolerance, meaning they resist damage by a physical or magical attack. Give the appropriate Chat Command so the party doesn't waste SP with ineffective attacks and/or magic.

Status Effects

The creatures in "The World" oftentimes utilize other powers to target their mental being or health. Depending on whether or not the malady infects the body (HP loss, poison, paralysis, etc.) or the mind (SP loss, sleep, confusion, etc.), the player will need to use an Antidote or Restorative. Antidotes and Restoratives also remove the effects of spells cast against one's physical and magical attributes.

RULING "THE WORLD"

The following section details the importance of keywords, the many facets of the Spring of Myst, the powers of the bracelet, and the numerous ways to acquire items. Last, but not least, tips on communicating within the world are provided to help lessen the chance of your online experience being one of loneliness and sorrow.

Color Coded Gems

When keywords affect the same modifier, they are each given a colored gem to indicate the order in which they are prioritized. Red takes precedence over green gems, which take precedence over the blue gems.

In other words, Red > Green > Blue.

Modifier Prioritization

When a single keyword affects multiple modifiers, they are ordered based on the following ranking. The letters shown in this list are found in the following tables under "Priority."

S > A > B > C > D > E > F

Keywords

Fully understanding the keyword-based area generation system may seem like a daunting task at first, but those who master its intricacies will be able to construct an area to their exact specifications. The first thing to learn is that areas are created by three keywords: Part A, Part B, and Part C. When a word is selected, various gems will appear in a grid to indicate which modifier that word is impacting. Since some words affect the same modifier, a ranking system has been incorporated to prioritize the words.

While the colored gems help determine whether Part A, Part B, or Part C is the controlling factor for each modifier, the modifiers themselves are ranked in terms of importance as well. This is a ranking that determines the order in which the modifiers become affected by a given keyword.

Modifier Descriptions

- **Field Type:** Determines the field's environment. There are 11 types: Scorching 1 & 2, Desert 1 & 2, Jungle, Snow 1 & 2, Wilderness, Earth, Leaf Mold, and Grassland.

- **Dungeon:** Controls the number of floors and rooms in the dungeon. Dungeons can have three to five floors. If the keyword has no Dungeon modifier, the dungeon will have three floors. Those with a value of 6 or 7 have four floors, whereas values of 8 to 10 yield a dungeon with five floors.

- **Weather:** This value determines the weather on the field, which has a direct role in determining the element of the area. One to three weather types are combined to determine the area's weather. The possibilities are: afternoon, evening, night, clouds, rain, thunder, snow, and blizzard.

- **Flatness:** Determines whether the field is flat, hilly, or steep.

- **Buildings:** Determines how many objects are scattered across the field. This value has three settings: few, normal, or many.

- **Area Level:** Determines the level of the monsters on the field and in the dungeon. The higher the number, the more powerful the monsters will be.

- **Monsters:** Dictates the level of the monsters in the area. The higher the number the more difficult the monsters will be. This further modifies the Area Level setting.

- **Items:** Dictates the value of the items discovered in the area. The higher the number, the more valuable the items in the area.

- **Magic Portals:** The final modifier determines the number of Magic Portals on the field and in the dungeon. The higher the number, the more Magic Portals there are.

The field type, weather, and monsters present all play a part in dictating what the overall element of the area will be. Regardless of the area's element, the player can expect to not encounter monsters whose element is directly opposite the overall element. Similarly, those creatures with an element that is the same as that of the area will show up in greater abundance.

FIELD TYPE ELEMENT NOTE

Field Type	Element	Note
Wilderness	Earth	
Snow 1 & 2	Water	
Scorching 1 & 2	Fire	
Desert 1 & 2	Fire	
Jungle	Water	When snow is present, this becomes Thunder element.
Leaf Mold	Water	When snow is present, this becomes Thunder element.
Grassland	Water	When thunder is present, this becomes a Thunder element.
Earth	Darkness	When thunder is present, this becomes a Thunder element.

TABLES EXPLAINED

Keyword	Keyword used in the area generation.
Priority	Priority Level for being selected.
Weather	Weather on the field.
Hills	Hilliness of the landscape in the field.
Buildings	Number of structures on the field.
Area Level	Area difficulty.
Obtained	Where the keyword was obtained. Those marked as "Start" are available at the beginning of the game, "Event" keywords are obtained through events such as cinematics, while "Other" indicates they were learned via the Board or Email.
Field	Indicates the type of field environment.
Dungeon	Dungeon size.
Monster	Modification to type of monsters present in the area.
Item	Relative value of the items found in the area.
Magic Portals	Number of Magic Portals on the field and in the dungeon.

PART A KEYWORDS

Keyword	Priority	Weather	Hills	Bldgs.	Area Lvl.	Obtained
Bursting	A	N/A	N/A	Normal	+1	Event
Hidden	A	N/A	N/A	Few	+1	Event
Expansive	A	N/A	N/A	Normal	+2	Event
Boundless	A	N/A	N/A	Many	+2	Event
Closed	A	N/A	N/A	Normal	+3	Event
Quiet	A	N/A	N/A	Few	+3	Event
Plenteous	A	N/A	N/A	Many	+3	Event
Collapsed	A	N/A	N/A	Normal	+4	Event
Cursed	A	N/A	N/A	Few	+4	Event
Buried	A	N/A	N/A	Many	+4	Event
Lonely	A	N/A	N/A	Few	+5	Event
Great	A	N/A	N/A	Normal	+5	Event
Chosen	A	N/A	N/A	Many	+5	Event
Discovered	D	Afternoon	Steep	N/A	N/A	Start
Indiscreet	D	Evening	Flat	N/A	N/A	Start
Putrid	D	Night	Hilly	N/A	N/A	Start
Hideous	D	Cloudy	Steep	N/A	N/A	Start
Soft	D	Rainy Afternoon	Flat	N/A	N/A	Start
Beautiful	D	Rainy Night	Hilly	N/A	N/A	Start
Raging	D	Stormy Afternoon	Flat	N/A	N/A	Start
Noisy	D	Stormy Night	Flat	N/A	N/A	Start
Dog Dancing	D	Blizzard Afternoon	Hilly	N/A	N/A	Start
Rejecting	D	Blizzard Night	Steep	N/A	N/A	Start
Sleepy	D	Afternoon	Flat	N/A	N/A	Start
Sinking	D	Evening	Hilly	N/A	N/A	Start
Chronicling	S	N/A	N/A	N/A	N/A	Other
Voluptuous	D	Clouds	Flat	N/A	N/A	Other
Detestable	D	Rainy Afternoon	Hilly	N/A	N/A	Other

PART B KEYWORDS

KEYWORD	PRIORITY	FIELD	MONSTERS	ITEMS	MAG. PORTALS	OBT.
Passed Over	B	N/A	-10	-10	N/A	Event
Forbidden	B	N/A	-8	-8	N/A	Event
Haunted	B	N/A	-6	-6	N/A	Event
Corrupted	B	N/A	-4	-4	N/A	Event
Oblivious	B	N/A	-2	-2	N/A	Event
Eternal	B	N/A	0	0	N/A	Event
Smiling	B	N/A	+2	+2	N/A	Event
Momentary	B	N/A	+4	+4	N/A	Event
Despaired	B	N/A	+6	+6	N/A	Event
Pagan	B	N/A	+7	+7	N/A	Event
Silent	B	N/A	+8	+8	N/A	Event
Distant	B	N/A	+9	+9	N/A	Event
Hopeless	B	N/A	+10	+10	N/A	Event
Primitive	E	Scorching 1	N/A	N/A	Normal	Start
Gluttonous	E	Scorching 2	N/A	N/A	Many	Start
Hot-Blooded	E	Desert 1	N/A	N/A	Few	Start
Destroyer's	E	Desert 2	N/A	N/A	Normal	Start
Solitary	E	Jungle	N/A	N/A	Many	Start
Someone's	E	Snow 1	N/A	N/A	Few	Start
Her	E	Snow 2	N/A	N/A	Normal	Start
Law's	E	Wilderness	N/A	N/A	Many	Start
Talisman	E	Earth	N/A	N/A	Few	Start
Orange	E	Leaf Mold	N/A	N/A	Normal	Start
Organ Market	E	Grassland	N/A	N/A	Many	Start
Agonizing	E	Scorching 1	N/A	N/A	Few	Start
Geothermal	E	Scorching 2	N/A	N/A	Normal	Start
Golden	E	Desert 1	N/A	N/A	Few	Other
Passionate	E	Desert 2	N/A	N/A	Few	Other

PART C KEYWORDS

KEYWORD	PRIORITY	FIELD	DUNGEON	WEATHER	OBTAINED
Aqua Field	C	Grassland	N/A	Afternoon	Event
Holy Ground	C	Snow 1	N/A	Clouds	Event
Sea of Sand	C	Desert 2	N/A	Afternoon	Event
Fort Walls	C	Wilderness	N/A	Clouds	Event
Twin Hills	C	Grassland	N/A	Stormy Night	Event
White Devil	C	Snow 2	N/A	Night	Event
Hypha	C	Leaf Mold	N/A	Afternoon	Event
Spiral	C	Wilderness	N/A	Rainy Afternoon	Event
Paradise	C	Earth	N/A	Clouds	Event
Fiery Sands	C	Desert 1	N/A	Evening	Event
Great Seal	C	Scorching 1	N/A	Night	Event
Fertile Land	C	Earth	N/A	Rainy Afternoon	Event
Nothingness	C	Wilderness	N/A	Clouds	Event
Melody	F	N/A	+6	N/A	Start
Remnant	F	N/A	+7	N/A	Start
March	F	N/A	+8	N/A	Start
Giant	F	N/A	+9	N/A	Other
Touchstone	F	N/A	+10	N/A	Other
Sunny Demon	F	N/A	+1	N/A	Other
Messenger	F	N/A	+2	N/A	Other
Scent	F	N/A	+3	N/A	Other
New Truth	F	N/A	+4	N/A	Other
Gate	F	N/A	+5	N/A	Other
Pilgrimage	F	N/A	+6	N/A	Other
Scaffold	F	N/A	+7	N/A	Other
Far Thunder	F	N/A	+8	N/A	Other
Tri Pansy	F	N/A	+9	N/A	Other
Treasured Gem	F	N/A	+10	N/A	Other

Spring of Myst

Many of the areas will have a mystical pond in the field known as a Spring of Myst. When Kite approaches a Spring of Myst, he can throw in a piece of armor or a weapon. Depending on the level of Monsieur or Grandpa (who resides in the Spring) and the current weather, Kite may get a better item in return. After throwing in the item, the spirit of the Spring rises and asks what it was that was thrown in. Kite can reply that it

was a "Golden Axe," "Silver Axe," or "Neither." If Kite throws in too powerful of an item (determined by the following tables) and selects "Neither," he will get his item back along with a Golden Axe and Silver Axe. If he selects either of the axes, his item is transformed into whichever axe Kite had chosen.

Weather's Influence on Level Change

Weather	Result When "Neither" is Chosen
Afternoon	Weapons +2 levels, Armor -1 level
Clouds	Weapons +2 levels, Armor -1 level
Night	Weapons +1 level, Armor +1 level
Evening	Weapons +1 level, Armor +1 level
Rain	Weapons -1 level, Armor +2 levels
Thunder	-1 level, Armor +2 levels
Snow	-1 level, Armor +2 levels

Weapons Upgrade Limits

Weap. Class	Monsieur Level 1	Monsieur Level 2	Grampa Level 1	Grampa Level 2
Twin Blade	4	11	7	14
Blademaster	4	11	7	14
Heavy Blade	4	12	7	15
Heavy Axeman	4	12	7	15
Long Arm	4	11	7	14
Wavemaster	4	10	6	13

Armor Upgrade Limits

Weap. Class	Monsieur Level 1	Monsieur Level 2	Grampa Level 1	Grampa Level 2
Head	8	26	16	32
Body	8	26	16	32
Hands	8	26	16	32
Feet	8	26	16	32

Where are the Springs of Myst?

Springs of Myst only appear in the following fields: Desert, Earth, Wilderness, Leaf Mold, and Grassland.

Upgrade Limits

The numbers presented in the preceding tables show the maximum level of weapon that can be achieved through upgrading at the Spring of Myst. It's important to toss in an item that doesn't exceed these limits; if this is ignored, Monsieur and Grampa won't be able to do anything with the items.

VIRUS CORES NOT FOUND

The vast majority of the Virus Cores aren't included in this volume of *.hack*. Kite will have all of the requisite Virus Cores when he needs them if he completes each of the areas in the order that they appear in this book.

The Bracelet

Kite's bracelet is without a doubt the single most important item in the game— fortunately, there's no way for him to lose it! As it stands, the bracelet has two functions: *Data Drain* and *Gate Hacking*. As Kite uses the bracelet to Data Drain enemies (especially bosses), he will acquire Virus Cores. The Virus Cores (labeled A through Z) are used to hack into areas that are otherwise off-limits to players. Kite can amass large numbers of the very common Virus Cores (A, B, and C) by Data Draining small, medium, and large monsters. However, the other 23 varieties of Virus Core are only found through events and by destroying bosses.

Whereas the Gate Hacking ability is rather straightforward and danger-free, the Data Drain ability is much more complex. Each time Kite uses the bracelet to Data Drain an enemy, he becomes more infected by a virus. As the infection becomes more powerful, the odds of a serious side-effect occurring increases.

Kite must balance his Data Drain usage and the virus so that the infection rate is kept low enough to not hinder his performance. Fortunately, there is a meter in the "Skills" menu that shows the current level of infection. As this meter changes from blue to green to yellow to red, the threat level increases and the chance of an adverse side effect increases along with it. The rate at which the virus spreads is linked to the disparity between Kite's level and that of the monster being Data Drained—much like the way in which EXP is awarded.

CONTAINING THE VIRUS

Each time Kite kills an enemy without using the Data Drain power, the infection rate drops by a random amount between 1 and 3 percentage points.

VIRUS INFECTION RATE

DIFFERENCE IN LEVEL	INFECTION RATE INCREASE
-5 or less	+7
-4	+7
-3	+8
-2	+9
-1	+10
0	+11
+1	+12
+2	+13
+3	+14
+4	+15
+5	+16
+6	+17
+7	+18
+8	+19
+9	+20
+10 or more	+20

As the virus spreads throughout Kite's body, the chance that a "Wild Glitch" will occur increases with each use of the bracelet. Wild Glitches can be positive, although most often their affect is negative. The odds of a Wild Glitch occurring are 50% of the current Virus Infection Rate. For example, if the current Infection Rate is 20%, there is a 10% chance of a Wild Glitch occurring. Similarly, if the infection spreads to 95% or higher, there is almost a 50% chance of something grave happening the next time the bracelet is used. When a Wild Glitch does occur, one of 16 different side effects will occur at random depending on the current Infection Rate.

VIRUS INFECTION RATE AND ASSOCIATED WILD GLITCHES

0-24% (Blue)	25-49% (Blue-Green)	50-74% (Green)	75-99% (Yellow)	100% (Red)
Everyone's HP & SP Restored	Everyone's HP & SP Restored	Everyone's HP & SP Restored	Everyone's HP & SP Restored	Everyone's HP & SP Restored
Everyone's HP & SP Restored	Magical Attack Down	Poison	Paralysis	All Poisoned
Physical Attack Down	Magical Defense Down	Paralysis	Sleep	All Paralyzed
Physical Defense Down	Magical Accuracy Down	Slow	All Poisoned	All Slow
Physical Accuracy Down	Poison	Charmed	All Paralyzed	All Charmed
Magical Attack Down	Paralysis	Confusion	All Paralyzed	All Confused
Magical Defense Down	Slow	Sleep	All Slow	All Sleep
Magical Accuracy Down	Charmed	All Poisoned	All Charmed	All Cursed
Poison	Confusion	All Paralyzed	All Confused	Everyone Loses 50% HP
Paralysis	Sleep	All Paralyzed	All Sleep	Everyone Loses 50% SP
Slow	Cursed	All Slow	All Sleep	Lose 1000 EXP
Charmed	All Paralyzed	All Sleep	All Cursed	Lose 1000 EXP
Confusion	All Sleep	All Cursed	Everyone Loses 50% HP	Everyone's HP & SP to 1
Sleep	Everyone Loses 50% HP	Everyone Loses 50% HP	Everyone Loses 50% SP	Everyone's HP & SP to 1
Cursed	Everyone Loses 50% SP	Everyone Loses 50% SP	Lose 800 EXP	Lose 1 Item
Lose 200 EXP	Lose 400 EXP	Lose 600 EXP	Everyone's HP & SP to 1	System Error

Item Gathering

The characters in "The World" are allowed to carry up to 40 different types of items and weapons, and up to 99 of each type. Additionally, characters can store up to 99 items at the Elf's Haven in Root Town. With capacities as large as this, it should be no surprise to learn that there are a number of different ways to acquire items.

The most common way to acquire items is by opening the Treasures and Risky Treasures in the fields and dungeons. Also, it is common for enemies to leave behind a Treasure after being killed (the Data Drain will also help to acquire valuable items). Regular Treasure chests carry common items (such as Health Drinks and low-level scrolls), while Risky Treasures often contain more valuable items (such as elemental potions and weapons and armor).

Treasures aren't the only objects in the game that yield items. When traveling through a dungeon, Kite can smash countless numbers of objects like Wooden Boxes, Jars, Urns, Eggs, and Barrels. While not all of these objects will yield an item, many do. Smashing things in a dungeon is one of the best ways to acquire element-based potions (such as Well Water and Burning Oil, as well as Health Drinks and Restoratives).

SYSTEM ERROR

The most severe penalty for allowing the virus to spread to 100% is the System Error. When this occurs, the user's system crashes and their game ends.

WARNING

Risky Treasures require a Fortune Wire to open. Without one, Kite runs the risk of exposing himself to the random dangers of the Treasure's trap. This is often a Death charge that extracts 50% of Kite's HP, while other times it can be a poison that causes the gradual loss of HP over time. Fortunately, Kite will receive a Fortune Wire if he opens a Risky Treasure without one, thereby ensuring that he doesn't have to suffer the penalty again.

KEY ITEMS

In addition to the standard Items Screen in the Personal Menu, there is also a Key Items Screen. Key Items include Books of Ryu, Grunty Food, Virus Cores, and Event Items. Each of these items can only be used at a specific time and place and are described elsewhere in this guide—some can't be used at all in this volume of *.hack*!

The two remaining ways to obtain items require something on Kite's part—no more freebies! One of these is through trading. Kite can trade with any of the PCs encountered in the Root Towns or even with his friends while at an area as long as they're not currently in battle. When trading for an item, Kite can offer the PC up to three different types of items and a quantity of up to 99 of each. Although the value of the items being offered differs from PC to PC (dependent on whether they can equip it or not), Kite can track the value of his offer by the four stars in the center of the trade screen. Each star represents 25% of the value of the item that Kite is trading for and will light up as he gets closer to making an offer the PC finds acceptable. Once the fourth star is lit, the trade can be executed. Please refer to the "Trade List" chapter of this guide for a complete list of all of the items available through trade.

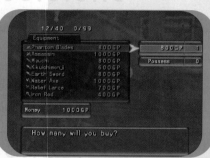

The final method of gathering items is through the Items, Magic, and Weapons shops located in each server's Root Town. Refer to the following tables for complete lists of every item available.

△ SERVER SHOPS

ITEM SHOP

ITEM	PRICE (GP)
Health Drink	100
Mage's Soul	500
Antidote	50
Restorative	50
Resurrect	300
Fortune Wire	10
Sprite Ocarina	100
Fairy's Orb	100
Warrior Blood	100
Knight Blood	100
Hunter Blood	100
Hermit Blood	100
Beast Blood	100
Wizard Blood	100

WEAPON SHOP

EQUIP.	PRICE (GP)
Phantom Blades	800
Assassin	1000
Mizuchi	800
Kikuichimonji	600
Earth Sword	800
Water Axe	1000
Relief Lance	700
Iron Rod	400

MAGIC SHOP

SCROLL	PRICE (GP)
Speed Charm	100
Light Cross	1000
Warrior's Bane	200
Knight's Bane	200
Hunter's Bane	200
Hermit's Bane	200
Beast's Bane	200
Wizard's Bane	200
Raining Rocks	200
Ice Storm	200
Fire Tempest	200
Green Gale	200
Lightning Bolt	200
Nightblight	200

θ SERVER SHOPS

ITEM SHOP

ITEM	PRICE (GP)
Health Drink	100
Mage's Soul	500
Antidote	50
Restorative	50
Resurrect	300
Fortune Wire	10
Sprite Ocarina	100
Fairy's Orb	100
Warrior Blood	100
Knight Blood	100
Hunter Blood	100
Hermit Blood	100
Beast Blood	100
Wizard Blood	100

WEAPON SHOP

EQUIP.	PRICE (GP)
Wooden Spear	1300
Electric Wand	1400
Steel Cap	800
Guard Cap	900
Face Guard	1000
Hiking Gear	1200
Wyrm Hide	1300
Grand Armor	1400
Silver Bracer	800
Silver Gloves	900
Silver Hands	1000
Ceramic Anklet	1200
Mountain Boots	1300
Mountain Guard	1400

MAGIC SHOP

SCROLL	PRICE (GP)
Speed Charm	100
Light Cross	1000
Warrior's Bane	200
Knight's Bane	200
Hunter's Bane	200
Hermit's Bane	200
Beast's Bane	200
Wizard's Bane	200
Raging Earth	200
Ice Floe	200
Meteor Swarm	200
Gale Breath	200
Plasma Storm	200
Dark Night	200

Communications

.hack//INFECTION may be a single-player RPG, but the game within the game, "The World," is brimming with dozens of other players and communicating with them is a big part of the game. The main way to communicate with the other players is to walk up to them and select the "Talk" option. Doing this is a nice way to see if that particular PC has a specific trade to offer or any gossip to spread. But since the other PCs are busy playing the game as well, they don't have time to provide Kite with detailed tips and suggestions. That's where the Board comes in!

The main way of gathering information from other players, whether it's tips on collecting Grunty Food or finding obscure sets of keywords, is by reading the countless discussions posted to the Board. The Board is the official forum for discussing "The World."

As Kite plays "The World" and develops relationships with other players, their affection for him will increase and they will contact him through email. Since Kite has to exit back to his desktop to check email, many of the conversations are about non-gaming topics. As shallow as it may seem, the main way to make friends online is by giving the other players valuable items and equipment. In short, valuable gifts cause large rises in affection.

GIFTS AND AFFECTION

VALUE OF GIFT	RISE IN AFFECTION
1 to 99 GP	+1
100 to 4999 GP	+10
5000 to 9999 GP	+20
10,000 to 19,999 GP	+50
> 20,000 GP	+10

FRIENDLY EMAILS

As the players Kite befriends become more and more comfortable with him, they will initiate conversational emails. Unlike emails that center around the gameplay, the player can choose between different replies to steer the conversation down different paths. Of course, if Kite decides to not reply to an email, he will be considered rude and won't likely get any more emails from that character. Similarly, if Kite answers with the correct reply, he not only continues the conversation, but increases that character's affection.

As an example of what to expect during gameplay, the following flowchart shows the correspondence between Kite and BlackRose, the character Kite is most likely to build a close friendship with. Note how certain responses lead to dead ends, while others lead to more discussion.

1 Subject: What do you... Requirement: Affection=50

Reply #1 How About You, Black Rose? Result Affection +10 → **3**

Reply #2 Well, Sometimes... Result Affection +10 → **2**

2 Subject: RE: Well, Sometimes... Requirement: Affection=75

Reply #1 Yeah, I've Done That Result

Reply #2 How About You, BlackRose? Result → **3**

3 Subject: RE: How About You, BlackRose? Requirement: Affection=100

Reply #1 A First Year...!? Result Affection +10 → **4**

Reply #2 That Rocks! Result Affection +10

4 Subject: RE: A First Year...!? Requirement: Affection=125

Reply #1 First I've Heard Result Affection +10

Reply #2 I'm a Middle-School Second Year... Result Affection +10 → **5**

5 Subject: RE: I'm a Middle-School Second-Year... Requirement: Affection=150

6 Subject: In the Beginning Requirement: Affection=175

Reply #1 Uh, That So? Result Affection +10

Reply #2 Hang in There! Result Affection +10

7 Subject: RE: Stuff Requirement: Affection=250, Complete the Game

CHARACTERS

PLAYABLE CHARACTERS

This chapter contains information on Kite, the main character in the game, as well as each of the players he befriends during his online adventures in "The World." Kite gets the opportunity to invite each of these characters to join him in his quest, at which time the player gains control of the entire party. Each character has different starting stats, as well as a different player class in "The World." Some characters, such as BlackRose, will befriend Kite almost instantly, while others are slower to make the connection. Either way, as their affection for Kite grows, they will each send emails to him to talk about non-gaming issues. By properly replying to these emails, Kite can learn about their real life including their age, real name, and where they're from!

KITE

CLASS	Twin Blade	
LEVEL	1	
HP	63	SP	13

STARTING STATS

	ATK	DEF	ACC	EVD
Physical	1.5	2.4	3.3	3.3
Magical	1.4	1.4	2.6	2.6

Earth	Water	Fire	Wood	Thunder	Darkness
1.2	1.2	1.2	1.2	1.2	1.2

Mind Resistance	Body Resistance
4.0	4.0

Kite is the central character in the game. He is a young middle school student who enters the online gaming arena under the tutelage of his friend Yasuhiko, a.k.a. Orca. When Orca suffers a tragic accident and lands in the hospital, it becomes Kite's charge to investigate the online game "The World" and discover a cure to his friend's illness.

Kite's kindness and skill as a gamer will net him many friends online. As Kite will see, these friends are his only allies against the powerful forces at work in "The World."

ORCA

CLASS	Blademaster	HP	1050
LEVEL	50	SP	160

Orca, Kite's friend, is the one who not only convinces Kite to start playing "The World," but he's also the character who Kite trusts the most. Orca takes Kite under his wing and helps teach him how to play the game. Unfortunately, Orca gets struck down by an infected monster in a low-level dungeon. Not only does his game character get destroyed, but the real-life Orca goes into a coma.

Orca is revered in "The World" by all those who know him. He and Balmung were known as the "Descendants of Fianna," which was the most powerful party found battling on the game's many servers. Orca was known for being very helpful to newbies and for showing lots of patience.

STARTING STATS

	Atk	Def	Acc	Evd
Physical	31	31	57	57
Magical	16	16	32	32

Earth	Water	Fire	Wood	Thunder	Darkness
16	0	0	0	0	0

Mind Resistance	Body Resistance
5	54

BLACKROSE

CLASS	Heavy Blade	HP	70
LEVEL	1	SP	13

Kite is anxious to make friends online and isn't too picky at first as he quickly latches on to BlackRose, a boisterous female with a sword as big as her ego. Kite meets this talkative player during his first trip online after the incident involving Orca. Although she is quick to give Kite a tongue-lashing for staring at her, she warms up to him before long and the two become good friends—especially once she admits to being a newbie too!

STARTING STATS

	Atk	Def	Acc	Evd
Physical	1.7	1.5	3.2	3.0
Magical	1.3	1.3	2.6	2.6

Earth	Water	Fire	Wood	Thunder	Darkness
0	0	1.2	0	0	0

Mind Resistance	Body Resistance
0.1	5.0

MISTRAL

CLASS	Wavemaster	HP	55
LEVEL	1	SP	20

Mistral is one of the most talkative players Kite encounters online. In addition to being a perky Wavemaster with great magical skills, she is in awe of Kite's magical bracelet and is always eager to join him in any adventure. Although Mistral always seems to be logged in and ready to answer an invite, the tribulations of life in the real world do get the better of her from time to time. It's not uncommon for her to suddenly log out of "The World" to tend to laundry or burnt dinners in the real world.

STARTING STATS

	Atk	Def	Acc	Evd
Physical	1.1	1.4	3.0	3.1
Magical	1.8	1.3	3.2	2.8

Earth	Water	Fire	Wood	Thunder	Darkness
0	0	0	0	1.3	0

Mind Resistance	Body Resistance
5	0.2

MIA

CLASS	Blademaster	HP	150
LEVEL	5	SP	25

Root Towns are known for having numerous players milling about at any given time, and it's not uncommon to get an earful of gossip while heading to the nearby magic shop. That is exactly how Kite learns of Mia, the mysterious cat-like female player. Mia is very skilled at only letting those around her know what she wants them to know—and not an ounce of information more. If this doesn't make her difficult to read as it is, the fact that she seldom responds to Flash Invitations makes it even more difficult to gauge her. Mia is seldom seen without Elk.

STARTING STATS

	Atk	Def	Acc	Evd
Physical	4.0	4.0	7.5	7.5
Magical	2.5	2.5	5.0	5.0

Earth	Water	Fire	Wood	Thunder	Darkness
0	2.5	0	0	0	0

Mind Resistance	Body Resistance
5.4	9.0

ELK

CLASS	Wavemaster	HP	85
LEVEL	3	SP	30

Of all the characters Kite meets during his time online, Elk is the least serious about playing "The World." In fact, Elk is much more concerned about the time he spends with Mia—and with making her his first real friend. Elk eventually becomes extremely jealous of Kite and seeks to limit the time Mia spends with him. As such, Elk doesn't spend a lot of time online and isn't there to join Kite's party too often.

STARTING STATS

	Atk	Def	Acc	Evd
Physical	1.3	2.2	5.0	5.3
Magical	3.4	1.9	5.6	4.4

Earth	Water	Fire	Wood	Thunder	Darkness
0	0	0	0	0	1.9

Mind Resistance	Body Resistance
7.0	0.6

PIROS

CLASS	Heavy Axeman	HP	125
LEVEL	3	SP	19

Piros is known as a true role-player. The person behind Piros is very interested in maintaining the integrity of the fantasy world depicted in "The World," and speaks as if he is from a different age. He wouldn't think of using slang and emotes to communicate with the other players. Piros is forever grateful of the playtime Kite shares with him and never refers to the boy by his name, but rather "he of fair eyes." As the only Heavy Axeman to befriend Kite, Piros is a valuable asset to any party.

STARTING STATS

	Atk	Def	Acc	Evd
Physical	3.4	2.2	5.9	4.4
Magical	1.6	1.9	3.8	3.8

Earth	Water	Fire	Wood	Thunder	Darkness
1.9	0	0	0	0	0

Mind Resistance	Body Resistance
0.3	7.0

NATSUME

CLASS	Twin Blade	HP	63
LEVEL	1	SP	13

Natsume is the consummate newbie. Not only is she obsessed with collecting weapons that are too strong for her current level, but she does not hesitate to beg and plead for other characters to give them to her. Fortunately, Natsume is a rather nice girl and spends enough time playing "The World" that she quickly levels up and becomes worthy of inclusion in one of Kite's parties.

STARTING STATS

	Atk	Def	Acc	Evd
Physical	1.5	1.4	3.3	3.3
Magical	1.4	1.4	2.6	2.6

Earth	Water	Fire	Wood	Thunder	Darkness
0	0	0	1.3	0	0

Mind Resistance	Body Resistance
0.1	5.0

GARDENIA

CLASS	Long Arm	HP	250
LEVEL	10	SP	40

Like Orca, Gardenia has quite a following and finds herself in the awkward position of having an unofficial fan club. As Kite finds out, this goes against her very serious demeanor. In fact, Kite can only convince her to talk to him by proving himself in battle. Despite her hard shell, Gardenia is an expert fighter and is the perfect addition to Kite's party—just don't expect to joke around too much when she's present!

STARTING STATS

	Atk	Def	Acc	Evd
Physical	8.0	5.0	14	14
Magical	4.0	5.0	8.0	8.0

Earth	Water	Fire	Wood	Thunder	Darkness
0	0	0	0	0	4.0

Mind Resistance	Body Resistance
1.0	14

SANJURO

CLASS	Heavy Blade	HP	350
LEVEL	15	SP	50

Kite meets Sanjuro in a way not too different from how he meets Natsume—he wants something that Kite has. Despite Kite's generosity and will to hand over the desired Kotetsu sword to the quiet stranger, Kite never learns too much about this sword-wielding soldier. Although Sanjuro is quite a force in battle, his true powers (and personality) are to remain a mystery until a future volume in the series.

STARTING STATS

	Atk	Def	Acc	Evd
Physical	11.5	8.5	20	17
Magical	5.5	5.5	11	11

Earth	Water	Fire	Wood	Thunder	Darkness
0	0	0	5.5	0	0

Mind Resistance	Body Resistance
1.5	19

NON-PLAYABLE CHARACTERS

BALMUNG

Balmung is Orca's partner in the Descendants of Fianna and is immediately skeptical of Kite's story. Balmung is one of the strongest characters in "The World" and, despite being a friend of Orca's, isn't ready to offer Kite his assistance. There are more questions than answers surrounding this arrogant, untrusting character.

AURA

There are few mysteries in "The World" stranger than that involving "the girl" known as Aura. The Board is abuzz with sightings of this ghost-like character, yet no one seems to know if she's a player, an in-game creature, or something else. Whoever she is, she certainly plays a key role in Kite's eventual possession of the bracelet and could possibly help bring Orca back to life. Or could she…?

HELBA

 XXX   XXX

****************MESSAGE DELETED**************

A JOURNEY WITH BLACKROSE

After a brief attempt at speaking with Orca in the hospital, Kite learns that the CC Corporation has emailed its registered users alerting them that the servers have been temporarily shut down and play will be limited to the Δ and Θ Servers. After learning this, click "The World" icon to access the game's title screen. Kite then posts a message on the Board titled "Coma" in hopes that someone from CC Corporation may see it and provide some friendly advice. There aren't any new posts to the Board and "The World" is currently offline for maintenance, so exit to the desktop.

Another email appears when Kite returns from posting on the Board. Although the image in the corner of the email resembles the girl Orca and Kite met online, her message is scrambled and unreadable for the most part. Nevertheless, there is mention of the book that was given to Kite and the last two lines seem to read, "There is no time. Please help me."

There's no way to tell how Kite is supposed to help the girl, but it's certain to involve "The World." With the game back online, log in and return to Aqua Capital Mac Anu. Upon arriving in Root Town, Kite meets a sexy, albeit boisterous, character named BlackRose. Kite's bashfulness and inexperience in online games doesn't exactly make for great conversation and the girl with the enormous sword storms off toward the bridge in the center of town.

OTHER PLAYERS' POSSESSIONS

Each player-character in the game has a set list of items that they are willing to trade. You can eventually unlock various secrets by meeting and trading with more and more people while in the towns. Since the other players aren't always online at the same time, it's best to talk to every new face that you encounter. There's no telling if you'll see them again.

Spend some time getting familiar with the town and its people. Use the Steel Blades and/or Yellow Candy to trade for the Shadow Blades (Hayate), Fuse Blades (Benkei), or Lath Blades (Mayunosuke). The Shadow Blades are level 6 weapons, the most powerful that Kite can obtain at this stage of the game. Kite may need to "trade up" for more valuable weapons before offering Hayate a deal she can't refuse.

Head to the item shop and purchase additional Health Drinks and at least 10 Fortune Wires. Also, if Kite has enough GP, purchase several Antidotes and a Sprite Ocarina as well. By and large, most of the items at this particular shop should be considered standard issue; don't venture into battle without an abundance of each one.

Return to the Chaos Gate after exploring the town. Upon arriving, BlackRose rushes up and offers to share some interesting keywords as long as Kite agrees to tag along. Agree to join her to receive BlackRoses's member address, as well as the keywords Δ: **Hidden, Forbidden, Holy Ground**. Add BlackRose to Kite's party, then select the keywords from the word list at the Chaos Gate.

Δ: Hidden, Forbidden, Holy Ground

RECOMMENDED PARTY: KITE AND BLACKROSE

Although this next area is Level 6, BlackRose should offer plenty of protection for the newbie Twin Blade. As it turns out, the area is not a typical field area with a dungeon, but rather the location of an intimidating cathedral. The two are then met by a lowly Goblin, and BlackRose cowers in the corner while Kite dispatches the weak foe.

AREA VITALS	
BATTLE LEVEL:	6
ELEMENT:	Water
GRUNTY FOOD:	N/A
ENVIRONMENT:	Cathedral
WEATHER:	N/A

ITEMS
Virus Core M

While the two study the statue in chains at the front of the cathedral, another player named Balmung storms in and orders them to leave just as a disruption in the network begins to occur. Balmung quickly slashes through the creature that appears, only to reveal a green glowing entity under the creature's skin. A computer virus has infected the network and is rewriting the data to form creatures with infinite HP!

Just as Kite experiences flashbacks of Orca, the voice of the girl is heard telling him to open the book. Kite follows her instructions and uses the Book of Twilight. He then becomes the possessor of a powerful bracelet that grants him the power to drain creatures of their data. This **Data Drain** attack is the only known way to defeat creatures possessing infinite HP. Slaying the beast yields **Virus Core M**.

A JOURNEY WITH BLACKROSE

RETURN TRIPS

Remember the address of the cathedral. You will make return trips here later in the game to uncover some of "The World's" secrets.

Balmung is less than impressed by Kite's actions and swears to kill Kite, as he believes it is Kite who has infected "The World" with this horrible virus. Outside, Balmung is met by a hacker named Helba and is told that Kite is in fact a friend of Orca, Balmung's partner.

Upon arriving back at Aqua Capital Mac Anu, head down the steps to the Recorder and save your game. Press the △ button to access the Personal Menu and Log Out of the game to return to the title screen.

A Search for More Information

A check of the Board reveals that Kite's message has been deleted—certainly an odd occurrence given its seriousness. Perhaps the moderator thought it was a hoax? Nevertheless, someone by the name of Stehoney has posted a challenge. The "Goblin Tag" challenges are covered in more detail in the "Side Quests" chapter later in the book. Exit back out to the desktop after reading Stehoney's post.

✉ **Thread: Let's Play Tag**
Post: Challenge Gob!   **Author: Stehoney**

Hello everybody.

I'm Stehoney the Golden Goblin gob. If you win tag against me, I'll give you a reward. Though that probably won't happen gob. Good luck gob.

Oh forgot something important gob. Stehoney is at: △: Detestable, Golden, Sunny Demon.

Come alone gob!

BlackRose sends Kite an email inviting him to contact her. Kite has several options in replying to her email. Since online RPGs emphasize group play, it's important to cultivate relationships with other players. The best way to do this is by making friends with them offline too! Rather than ignore BlackRose's email, accept her offer to help and send her the reply titled "Thanks."

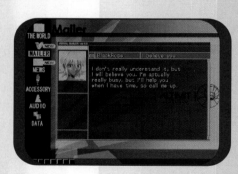

The second email is from Helba, the peculiar woman seen talking to Balmung outside the cathedral. She provides Kite with additional information regarding his bracelet and its Data Drain ability. After reading the emails, check the news program to learn about a strategy guide that is being published to help gamers succeed in playing "The World"—they say it's full of expert strategy and valuable data… but you already knew that!

Log back into "The World" and return to Aqua Capital Mac Anu on the Δ Server. As Kite arrives at the Chaos Gate, he overhears two other players discussing a character resembling a cat in the alleyway—a veritable alleycat. Head past the magic shop toward the alley where Elk and Mia are hanging out. Mia, the cat, will then inspect Kite's bracelet. Neither Kite nor Elk can see the bracelet, yet Mia can. There's obviously something different about Mia and the way in which she leaves gives rise to all sorts of suspicions.

GOBLIN TAG ROUND ONE

This is a good time to meet up with Stehoney and play his game of tag. Stehoney's challenge is just the first of five in which Kite can participate in. Refer to the "Side Quests" chapter for additional information.

Since the only other address Kite has is that which was given to him by Stehoney, there is little else he can do at this point to bring him closer to helping Orca. Log back out of the server and check the Board for new messages—maybe someone has posted some other newbie-friendly keywords?

The Board was quite active while Kite was logged into the game. Many of the new messages have valuable information, but make sure you read the following three especially to add the keywords to the Word List.

Thread: Is This an Event Character   **Author: TAO**
Post: Girl

I saw a strange character in the dungeon of: Δ: Expansive, Haunted, Sea of Sand.

It was a little girl with long hair, but it didn't look like another player. She was kind of white—like a ghost and moved without a sound. Oh, and the music might have stopped too!

I could be mistaken, but if anyone sees her, please tell me!

Thread: Protected Area   **Author: Waffle**
Post: I can't go in

I tried a random keyword, but a warning message came up and I couldn't go in. I think it was: Δ: Closed, Oblivious, Twin Hills.

Anyone know anything about it?

Thread: Increasing Levels   **Author: Korm**
Post: RE: Game Over!!

Depending on the area, the level of the enemy varies, so you have to find the area that's best suited for you. Area I recommend for beginners: Δ: Discovered, Primitive, Touchstone.

Monsters don't vary that much in level, so you won't die too quickly and see that dreadful GAME OVER screen. But there's 5 floors to this dungeon and the ones on the lower level are pretty strong, so just don't go all the way down.

You should probably raise your level to at least level 5 in the upper levels before you go down there.

GETTING
STARTED
ADVANCED
HACKING
CHARACTERS
WALKTHROUGH
SIDE QUESTS

AREA FOR BEGINNERS

Log back into "The World" and stock up on supplies at the various shops in Aqua Capital Mac Anu. Return to the Chaos Gate and invite BlackRose to join Kite in a trip to the area mentioned on the Board. This is the perfect place for newbies like Kite and BlackRose!

△: Discovered, Primitive, Touchstone

RECOMMENDED PARTY: KITE AND BLACKROSE

AREA VITALS

BATTLE LEVEL:	1
ELEMENT:	Fire
GRUNTY FOOD:	Snaky Cactus
	Bloody Egg
	Golden Egg
ENVIRONMENT:	Desert
WEATHER:	Cloudy

MONSTERS

FIELD:

Goblin: Earth
Mad Grass: Wood
Disco Knife

DUNGEON:

Deadly Moth
Disco Knife
Mad Grass: Wood
Magical Goblin: Fire
Chicken Hand: Wood
Sword of Chaos
Cadet Valkyrie: Wood

ITEMS

Bandana	Meteor Swarm
Leather Armor	The Hanged Man
Fire Tempest	Earth Sword
Leather Coat	Amateur Blades
Nomad's Hood	The Lovers
Virus Core A	Head Gear
The Death	Leather Gloves
Burning Oil	The Moon
Brigandine	Virus Core B
Antidote	Gakaku
Restorative	Wrist Band
Health Drink	Sprite Ocarina

GOTT STATUE ITEMS

Ceramic Anklet
Rainbow Card
Grunt Doll

Since this is your first real chance to explore an area to its fullest, it's important to be as thorough as possible. Also, take advantage of the opportunity to level up in a relatively safe environment. Use a Fairy's Orb to reveal all the Magic Portals in the field and spend as much time as it takes battling the enemies throughout the map. In addition to gaining valuable EXP, Kite will uncover numerous Treasures and Risky Treasures. Give any duplicate armor or Heavy Blade weapons to BlackRose, since she isn't as well equipped.

It's also a good idea to use the Data Drain skill as a finishing move. Once an enemy has lost the majority of its HP, it will go through a phase known as the Protect Break; this is when it becomes susceptible to the Data Drain. Not every enemy is vulnerable to the Data Drain, but those that are yield more valuable items and Virus Cores, which will be instrumental in Gate Hacking when the time arrives.

BlackRose's character class is geared toward intense combat, so it's best at this stage to leave the strategy set to Operation Wonder Battle. Inspect the various skills that BlackRose currently has equipped and memorize them. Keep an eye on each character's HP and issue the First Aid command if BlackRose has the Repth recovery skill. Also, utilize the Burning Oils to bolster the party's fire rating.

RAISING
A GRUNTY

ADDITIONAL
ELEMENTS

TRADE
LIST

BOOKS
OF RYU

BESTIARY

Stop at the Spring of Myst and toss in one of the duplicate armors that you pick up. Tell Monsieur that it was a Golden Axe that was tossed in to get one in return. Collect as many Golden Axes as possible, because they are very valuable trading commodities.

Battle through all of the monsters to clear each of the field portals before entering the dungeon. Both Kite and BlackRose should reach Level 3 by simply leveling up on the field.

Dungeon, B1

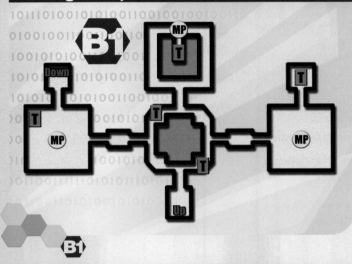

The first level of the dungeon features the same assortment of enemies as the field, an addition being the Deadly Moth. Data Drain the Deadly Moth for a chance at the **Earth Sword**. If you attain this weapon, give it to BlackRose to improve her attack rating.

Dungeon, B2

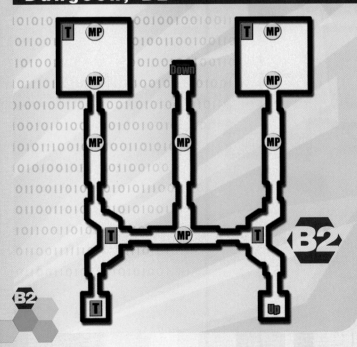

The second floor of the dungeon introduces Magical Goblins. These evasive members of the goblin family have a fire tolerance that negates any attacks from Fire-based skills or items. However, that's not their real strength. They are very fond of casting spells that cause a slow depletion of HP over time. Rush toward them and slash at them before they get a chance to cast their spells. If Kite or BlackRose gets struck with one of these spells, use an Antidote to cure the malady.

Dungeon, B3

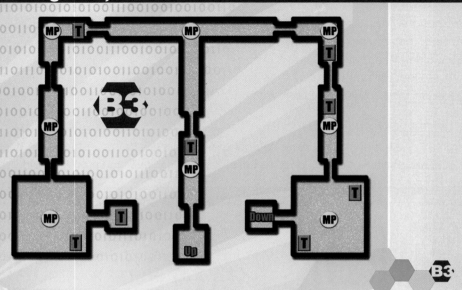

Dungeon, B4

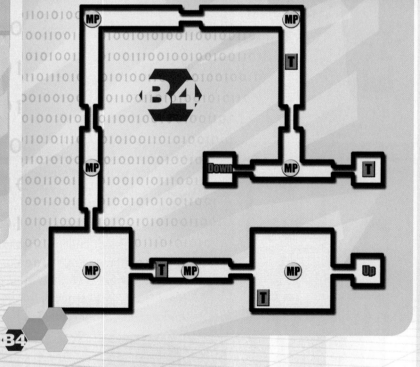

THE BRACELET IS SHINING!

By actively using the Data Drain to defeat enemies, you will reap an unexpected reward. For every 10 times the Data Drain is used, another Ryu Book will appear in the Book of 1000 screen of the Key Items menu. Ryu Books record an abundance of statistical data regarding gameplay, and provide the player with various unlockable secrets for progress.

The first room beyond the stairway contains several enemies, including a Sword of Chaos. Attempt to Data Drain this levitating sword and shield for a chance at the **Gakaku**. The Gakaku is a Level 3 weapon for members of the Blademaster class; it's one of the less common weapons, too.

RAISING
A GRUNTY

ADDITIONAL
ELEMENTS

TRADE
LIST

BOOKS
OF RYU

BESTIARY

Dungeon, B5

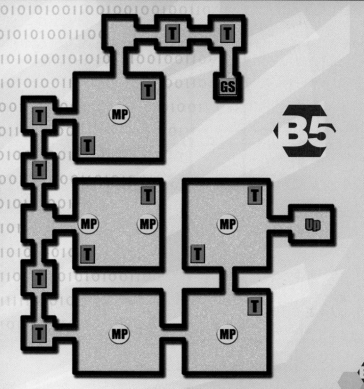

The fifth and final floor contains yet another new type of enemy, the Cadet Valkyrie. These axe-carrying soldiers are more deadly than the other enemies encountered thus far, but an Earth-based skill or spell will put them down with ease. From this point on, it's extremely important to keep an eye on the party's HP, as each new enemy is more deadly than the last.

Continue to progress through the dungeon to the Gott Statue and lay claim to the three items in the Treasure. The **Ceramic Anklet** is a Level 11 light armor, so immediately equip it. Use the **Sprite Ocarina** to return to the field, then warp back to town. Upon returning to Aqua Capital Mac Anu, put the duplicate armor and weapons to work by trading and selling the items to any of the shopkeepers. Consider storing one of each item at the Elf's Haven just in case the item is need-ed in the future. Save your game and stock up on Fortune Wires and recovery items.

Gift Giving

It's important to think of Kite *and* BlackRose's needs when looking to trade with other player-characters. After all, the stronger she is, the better your chances for survival. Not to mention, there's no better way to win her affection than by presenting her with a high-level weapon! Consider tracking down Mackey and trading for the Slayer sword on BlackRose's behalf.

CHASING THE GIRL

Give the "Everyone Gather" command to make BlackRose return to the Chaos Gate and give her any items that benefit those in the Heavy Blade class, such as the Slayer sword and Hands of Earth hand armor. Have her follow Kite to the Recorder to save the game, then return to the Chaos Gate and select the set of keywords that go to the area where the girl was seen.

△: EXPANSIVE, HAUNTED, SEA OF SAND

RECOMMENDED PARTY: KITE AND BLACKROSE

AREA VITALS

BATTLE LEVEL:	3
ELEMENT:	Fire
GRUNTY FOOD:	Oh No Melon
ENVIRONMENT:	Desert
WEATHER:	Clear

MONSTERS

FIELD:
Swordmanoid: Thunder
Magical Goblin: Fire
Deadly Moth

DUNGEON:
Chicken Hand: Wood
Swordmanoid: Thunder
Magical Goblin: Fire
Deadly Moth

ITEMS

Head Gear	Fire Tempest
Virus Core B	Health Drink
Phantom Blades	Restorative
Steel Blades	Burning Oil
Mage's Soul	Leather Gloves
The Devil	Resurrect
Sandals	Battle Axe
Virus Core A	Antidote
Resurrect	Meteor Swarm
Safety Shoes	Guard Cap
The Hanged Man	Steel Cap
Used Greaves	The Lovers

GOTT STATUE ITEMS

Cougar Bandana
Grunt Doll
Yellow Candy

TIME WILL HEAL ALL WOUNDS

Well, maybe not *all* wounds, but it will heal the magical maladies inflicted by the goblins. Because Kite and BlackRose have a relatively high HP limit, they won't be in mortal danger if they run out of Antidotes. Simply let the effects of the spells wear off over time and use the Repth skill or strengthening items to counter the status abnormalities.

Kite meets another player upon entering the field. Supposedly, an operator said that the area was unplayable so everyone must return to town. While this may be true for those unaware of the strange occurrences going on inside "The World," Kite and BlackRose know better than to turn away without further investigation. Use a Fairy's Orb to reveal the locations of the Magic Portals, then scour the map to level up.

Since the party's experience level is double that of the combat rating for this area, the monsters shouldn't pose a significant threat. Nevertheless, many of the skirmishes will

include Magical Goblins; these creatures will use various weakening skills against Kite and BlackRose. Keep an eye on each player's status and use Antidote and Restorative potions if an ailment strikes. If you run low on these items, issue the "First Aid!" command to make BlackRose do some healing. Also, since Magical Goblins possess a Fire Tolerance, don't attack with a Fire-based skill or item.

The weather conditions in this area are just right for Monsieur to increase the level of an item tossed into the Spring of Myst. Toss in an unused weapon, then select "Neither" when asked what you've lost. For example, if you throw in the Phantom Blades (Level 2), you'll receive the Spark Blades (Level 3) in return.

RAISING
A GRUNTY

ADDITIONAL
ELEMENTS

TRADE
LIST

BOOKS
OF RYU

BESTIARY

Dungeon, B1

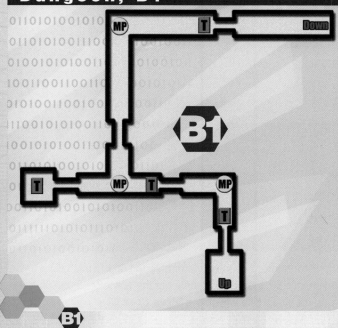

Kite and BlackRose meet an Administrator NPC inside the first room of the dungeon. Although the sentry character is

there to warn players that the area is unstable, you must continue onward. Simply walk around the administrator and enter the next room of the dungeon.

The dungeon contains the same monsters encountered in the field, the only new addition is the Chicken Hand. Continue fighting and use the Burning Oil to increase the

party's fire status. Smash all of the eggs in the westernmost room for additional supplies. Similarly, inspect the symbol in front of the staircase to gain an added buff.

Dungeon, B2

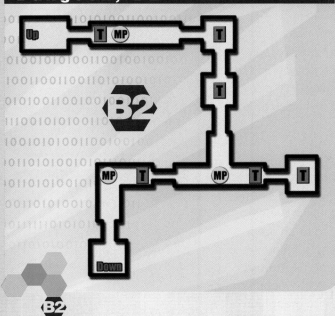

Dungeon, B3

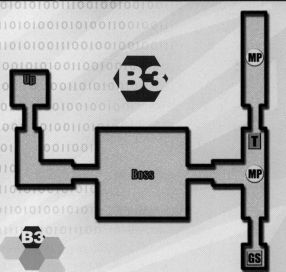

The doorway leading out of the second room on this floor is awash in a purple haze—a surefire indicator that what lies beyond is both large and unfriendly! Top off each party member's HP and SP, and use any strengthening skills or items now, especially if they're of the thunder element.

BOSS FIGHT: HEADHUNTER

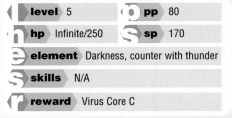

level	5	pp	80
hp	Infinite/250	sp	170
element	Darkness, counter with thunder
skills	N/A
reward	Virus Core C

Attack this beast just like any other monster you've encountered in the dungeon thus far. Issue the "Skills!" command to make BlackRose unleash her mighty physical attacks. Keep an eye on each member's health and have Kite attack with consecutive magical skills. Continue attacking until the beast suffers roughly 800 HP of damage.

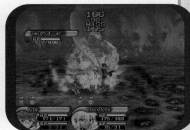

After taking substantial damage, the Headhunter becomes vulnerable to Data Drain. Use a Mage's Soul, if necessary, to replenish lost SP, then immediately put the bracelet to use. In addition to rewriting the virus-carrying creature, Kite will gain a **Virus Core C**.

After getting drained of the virus, the lowly Headhunter emerges with just around 250HP—barely more than Kite and BlackRose. Issue the "Skills!" command to BlackRose again and hack away at the Headhunter with Kite's weapons while BlackRose finishes off the beast.

COME AGAIN?

Oftentimes, Kite and his party members will automatically return to Root Town after defeating a boss. Unfortunately, this means they don't get to reach the Gott Statue or clear the dungeon of all Magic Portals. When this occurs, save your game at the Recorder and return to the area. The party can then clear the dungeon of Magic Portals and collect the items from the Gott Statue, if you so desire. Nevertheless, while this is beneficial to the party, it's not necessary.

This return trip is definitely worthwhile, because the Cougar Bandana is a Level 11 head armor that greatly increases Kite's ability to evade magic, and when equipped with the La Repth skill it enables Kite to heal the entire party with one casting!

After the boss fight, Kite and BlackRose encounter a female player-character named Mistral. Mistral is quite talkative but quickly logs out of the game to salvage her burnt dinner in the real world. Before she goes, she gives Kite her member address and asks him to invite her to his next adventure.

Back in Aqua Capital Mac Anu, Kite is met by a friendly player-character named Piros who seems to take RPGs too literally at times. He provides Kite with a set of keywords that lead to an area where Piros is planning on avenging a friend. He'd like Kite to go to Δ: **Indiscreet, Gluttonous, Pilgrimage** to watch Piros vanquish the monster that has harassed his friend. Agree to meet him there (you don't have to go right now); it will definitely benefit Kite in the long run.

PIROS'S WITNESS

Stock up on supplies and take a brief run through town to see if there are any new faces milling about. Trade for items that benefit the Wavemaster character class, as Mistral is a good choice to accompany Kite and BlackRose on the next adventure. When you're ready, return to the Chaos Gate and add Mistral to the party.

Although perhaps poorly equipped as far as a Wavemaster is concerned, Mistral is carrying some valuable items for those in other classes, specifically the Twin Blade. Seek out Crest in Root Town and trade with him to get the Air Wand. Then, trade the Air Wand to Mistral to get the Sotetsu, a Level 9 Twin Blade weapon that adds the "Critical Hit" effect. Give her any of Kite's unusable items and head off to the area designated by Piros.

> **WARNING!**
>
> Although it's important to help Mistral level up, remember that this area is a little more than she can handle right now. Bring plenty of Resurrects and give the "First Aid!" command often to help get her through to the end!

△: INDISCREET, GLUTTONOUS, PILGRIMAGE

RECOMMENDED PARTY: KITE, BLACKROSE, AND MISTRAL

AREA VITALS	
BATTLE LEVEL:	4
ELEMENT:	Earth
GRUNTY FOOD:	Golden Egg
	Immature Egg
ENVIRONMENT:	Wilderness
WEATHER:	Cloudy

MONSTERS

FIELD:
Deadly Moth
Magical Goblin: Fire
Sky Fish: Water

DUNGEON:
Sword of Chaos
Magical Goblin: Fire
Sky Fish: Water
Headhunter: Darkness
Hell Doberman: Fire

ITEMS

The Devil		Face Guard	0
Amateur Blades	1	Earth Sword	1
Curing Sword		Virus Core A	1
Guard Cap	0	Restorative	0
The Death		Fire Spear	0
The Fool	0	Well Water	0
Raging Earth		Antidote	0
Raining Rocks	1	Ring Mail	1

GOTT STATUE ITEMS

Hunter's Hood
Rainbow Card
Grunt Doll

Many of the enemies in this area should look familiar; they're easily slain by the two weapon-wielders. Mistral, on the other hand, has her work cut out for her just to survive. Since she's not cut out for physical battle, issue the "Skills!" command (if not specific commands) to her individually.

Depending on Kite's previous weapon, he may have encountered difficulty cutting down the Magical Goblins in a single strike. However, this is no longer a problem with the Sotetsu. Magical Goblins tend to target the weakest member of the party with weakening spells, so cut them down in a hurry to keep from having to use numerous Antidotes and Restoratives.

Although the wilderness landscape isn't conducive for Grunty Food or a Spring of Myst, sweep the field clear of Magic Portals to enable Mistral to gain valuable EXP. Doing so will elevate Mistral to a Level 4 Wavemaster before she even sets foot in the dungeon!

Dungeon, B1

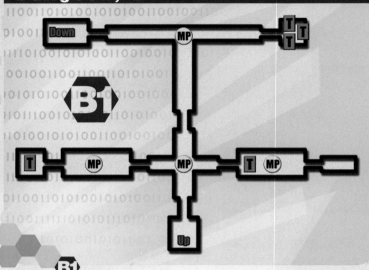

The first floor of the dungeon is the largest of the three and contains several notable items to pick up. Grab the **Golden Egg** in the southwestern hall en route to the room full of crates. Similarly, the room in the northeastern corner contains several Treasures, various breakables, and an **Immature Egg**.

Dungeon, B2

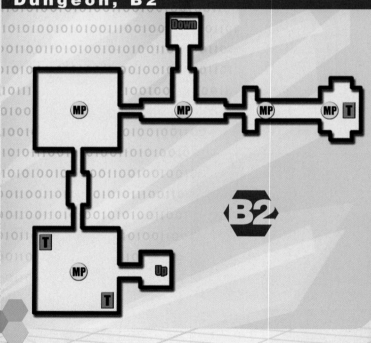

The first Magic Portal on this floor spawns a Headhunter as well as a couple of lesser creatures. Give the "Skills!" command to make Mistral and BlackRose attack the lesser enemies, and let Kite concentrate on the Headhunter. Use Kite's most powerful skill, the Flame Dance, to eliminate the creature in an instant. Additional Headhunters lie in wait throughout the dungeon. Use the Sotetsu to deliver swift punishment to them, and use Data Drain to acquire the **Fire Spear** weapon. You can sell it or trade it later.

Dungeon, B3

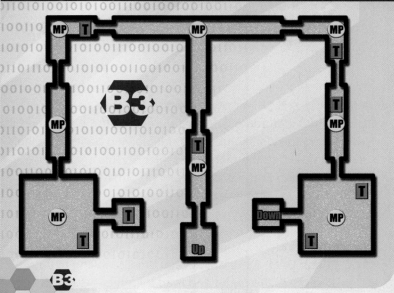

This dungeon is one of the few that you can completely explore before engaging in a boss battle or triggering an event. To do so, however, requires battling past a couple of Hell Dobermans. Since these creatures have a Fire Tolerance, the Flame Dance won't be of any help. Instead, use the Tiger Claws skill to slash away at them.

Travel east at the main intersection to open the last of the Dungeon Portals. Also, prepare to fight a Hell Doberman and a pair of Headhunters. This is the type of battle that Kite and BlackRose need to fight to help their friend Mistral gain EXP. The Gott Statue is in the room to the west of the intersection. When finished with these rooms, head north to find Piros.

Kite and his partners find Piros fighting a losing battle against a Rock Head enemy. Although Piros wants to avenge his friend without the help of outsiders, it's clear that he needs help.

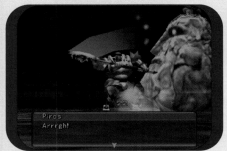

BOSS BATTLE: ROCK HEAD

level	9	pp	185
hp	410	sp	290
element	Earth, counter with Wood		
skills	Rig Saem		
reward	Meteor Strike		

The party can easily dismantle the Rock Head while the creature remains distracted by Piros. Issue the "Skills!" command and place any Wood-based skills or items to use with Kite. The Elemental Hit delivers twice the damage, thereby making the Rock Head's HP recovery magic irrelevant.

After the boss fight, Piros gives Kite the **Meteor Strike** scroll as well as his member address. After returning to town, visit the Elf's Haven shop to stash some items and sell the booty from the Gott Statue. Use the money to replenish Kite's supply of Antidotes and Fortune Wires, among other things. It's a good idea to trade away some duplicate weapons with Crest to gain the Wyrm Scale armor.

Although there is a set of keywords ready to use at the Chaos Gate, there are several emails waiting to be read. Log out of the game and read the email—especially the one from the CC Corporation!

YOU'VE GOT... FRIENDS!

Curious as to whether or not BlackRose and the others enjoy Kite's company? Well, as their affection for Kite grows, the other characters will start to send Kite friendly emails about everything from sports to food! Make sure you send a polite reply to continue nurturing the friendship and to learn more about their private lives. If time goes by without hearing from another player-character, it's because Kite isn't being friendly enough to them. Invite them on the next adventure and lavish them with gifts!

✉ Thread: CC Corporation
Subject: You're Our Winner!

0011001100110101000

Congratulations! You are the lucky winner of our One Year Anniversary, Power Up Campaign! As a prize, you will receive a special level up item created for this occasion. You will receive your prize at a shop in Root Town.

Return to Root Town after reading the emails and head to any shop to collect the **Book of Law**. This special item is unusable in this volume of the game, but will be an important item in one of the later installments.

Congratulations! You're the big winner of our contest! Please take your prize.

THE POWER OF THE BRACELET

Moments after collecting the Book of Law from one of the shops in town, Kite receives yet another email alert. Log out of "The World" and check the email program to read the message from Mia, as it reveals another set of keywords.

✉ **Thread: Mia**
Subject: Power of the Bracelet

Data Drain is not the only power on your bracelet. Do you want to know more?

You do, don't you? Δ: Boundless, Corrupted, Fort Walls. I'll be waiting at this area, so come alone.

Log back into the game and head straight for the Recorder to save your game before venturing off alone. Select Mia's keywords from the list at the Chaos Gate and warp to the area to meet up with her.

Δ: BOUNDLESS, CORRUPTED, FORT WALLS

RECOMMENDED PARTY: KITE

AREA VITALS	
BATTLE LEVEL:	7
ELEMENT:	Earth
GRUNTY FOOD:	Root Vegetable
	Immature Egg
	Golden Egg
ENVIRONMENT:	Wilderness
WEATHER:	Night

MONSTERS
FIELD:
Fiend Menhir: Thunder
Bee Army
Hob Goblin: Earth
DUNGEON:
Fiend Menhir: Thunder
Bee Army
Hob Goblin: Earth
Dust Curse
Shield Man: Darkness
Rock Head: Earth

ITEMS	
Virus Core B	Antidote
The Fool	Health Drink
Hiking Gear	The Devil
Resurrect	Silver Gloves
Lath Blades	Raining Rocks
Wind Axe	Well Water
Mage's Soul	Silver Bracer
Raging Earth	Thunder Axe
The Moon	Silver Hands
Grand Armor	Jungle Boots
Restorative	

GOTT STATUE ITEMS
Snow Panther
Rainbow Card
Yellow Candy

This quest marks Kite's first solo expedition and it's likely to be more difficult. Stock a large supply of Health Drinks, Antidotes, and Mage's Souls in your inventory for when things go awry. Also, trade with Mistral for the Sotetsu if it's not already in Kite's inventory. The Tiger Claw skill linked with this weapon greatly increases Kite's odds of surviving when battling against multiple enemies.

Although the first few battles will probably be quite tough, there is over 1,000 EXP to gain by killing every monster on the field. Similarly, you can gain an additional 1,000 EXP in the dungeon.

IT'S ALIVE!

The Fiend Menhir spins around several times while hovering off the ground when resurrecting a fallen enemy. Let this be your clue that what once was dead is now alive.

The majority of Magic Portals in the field contain multiple enemies; one of them is almost always a Fiend Menhir. These boulder-shaped beasts constantly resurrect other enemies. For this reason, it's important to focus attacks on the Fiend Menhir whenever it's present. Although the other monsters may have a more potent attack, you can't make any headway in these skirmishes as long as the Fiend Menhirs are alive. Since they possess lots of HP, use the Data Drain on them at the first opportunity.

Kite's best chance for clearing the field of all its enemies is to rush in between each group of monsters, let them draw in around him, then unleash the Tiger Claw skill attack. This whirling attack can inflict severe damage to every enemy within Kite's perimeter. Also, since it only costs 10 SP, Kite can perform the skill multiple times if necessary. Use Health Drinks instead of recovery skills to regain lost HP; this saves SP for the Tiger Claw.

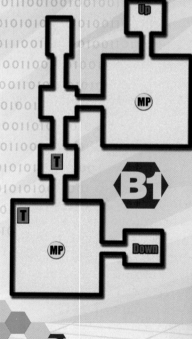

Dungeon, B1

When Kite makes it to the dungeon entrance, another Administrative NPC tells him to leave. However, Kite decides to ignore the warning and continues on in spite of it.

The first floor of the dungeon contains mostly the same enemies as outside in the field. Continue to rely on the Tiger Claw to beat them into submission. The dungeon contains several **Immature Eggs** and **Golden Eggs**, as well as a **Symbol**. Grab all of the items and don't miss an opportunity to smash a warrior's body or crate, as every extra Antidote and Health Drink will come in handy deeper in the dungeon.

Dungeon, B2

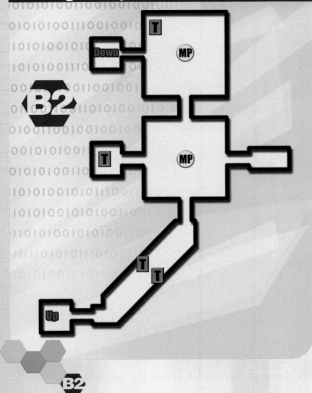

The first large room on the second floor contains a Shield Man and a couple of Bee Armies. The Shield Man may have a Darkness Tolerance, but it succumbs to the Tiger Claw just as easily as the rest. Work to the center of the room and take out all four monsters with a single Tiger Claw attack. Depending on Kite's current skill level, he can gain nearly 150 EXP from that single attack! Scour the adjacent rooms for supplies, then continue north toward the staircase.

Dungeon, B3

The battles start getting tougher on the dungeon's third floor. Not only does Kite have to battle against a former boss, but two of them at the same time! Use a Well Water item to increase Kite's Earth attribute when fighting the pair of Rock Heads. Keep a safe distance from them to avoid taking damage and use any Wood-based skills or items.

Dungeon, B4

Dungeon, B5

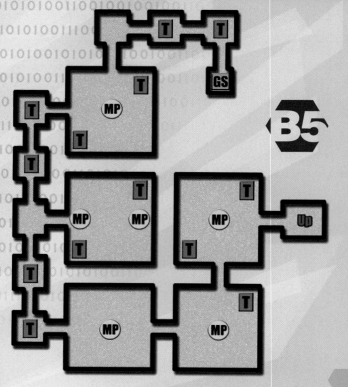

Mia's voice leads Kite into the depths of the dungeon and directly to a boss fight. Gain some extra supplies by sweeping the small rooms to the west and east before walking through the purple haze into the boss's lair. On the other side, Mia sends Kite toward the Magic Portal containing the beast.

BOSS BATTLE: RED WYRM

level 10	**pp** 105
hp Infinite/850	**sp** 620
element Fire, counter with Water	
skills Breath, Vak Don	
reward Virus Core M	

The Red Wyrm is a large winged creature capable of flipping forward and slapping Kite with its tail. Keep a safe distance away from it and run to the side when it begins to flip over. Although it's difficult to knock this creature into a state in which the Data Drain can be performed, it can be accomplished by keeping up a steady flow of skill and item attacks. Use the Tiger Claw immediately after the Red Wyrm attacks, but otherwise, stay away and use Raging Earth and Raining Rocks scrolls against it.

Since the creature is Fire-based, it's only natural that it can breathe fire. Use a Burning Oil to help offset the damage caused by this nasty attack, and use a Health Drink after being struck with this attack because Kite likely won't survive two in a row without any recovery. The beast's other attacking method is to slap its wings together on top of Kite. This attack is the least predictable, but doesn't deliver too much damage.

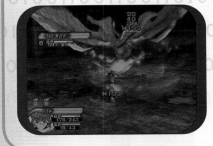

After enough damage has been inflicted, Data Drain the creature. Kite receives the valuable **Virus Core M** for his efforts, but still must finish off the Red Wyrm's remaining 850 HP. Continue attacking with the Tiger Claw and the various spell scrolls and monitor Kite's health closely. Kite can perform a second Data Drain on the Red Wyrm, but it isn't necessary and may not be worth the risk of spreading the virus—especially if Kite is low on health.

After the battle, Mia and Elk emerge from the shadows and inform Kite of the *other* ability his bracelet has—the ability to hack gates. Use the Virus Cores that Kite has been collecting to hack gates that block certain areas. With the bracelet and the right assortment of Virus Cores, Kite can pick the locks and go almost anywhere he chooses. Kite then follows Mia and Elk back to Root Town where they teach him this new ability. Save your game at the Recorder before joining them at the Chaos Gate.

COME AGAIN?

This is another area that Kite must return to if he wants to clear the dungeon of its Magic Portals and gain the items at the Gott Statue. Proceed with Kite and Mia to the next area, but return later with two other characters to help them level up.

PROTECTED AREA #1

Virus Core Requirements: 2 "M"

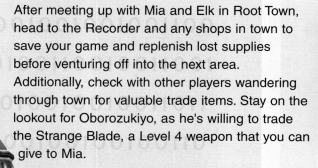

After meeting up with Mia and Elk in Root Town, head to the Recorder and any shops in town to save your game and replenish lost supplies before venturing off into the next area. Additionally, check with other players wandering through town for valuable trade items. Stay on the lookout for Oborozukiyo, as he's willing to trade the Strange Blade, a Level 4 weapon that you can give to Mia.

Return to the Chaos Gate and add Mia and Elk to Kite's party. Elk is a Level 3 Wavemaster and Mia is a Level 5 Blademaster, so it's apparent that wherever they go Kite will be the lead attacker.

As you prepare to enter the Chaos Gate, Mia tells Kite to select an address for a Protected Area—Kite was able to find one such address on the Board—but if he didn't read it, Mia will read it to him. Selecting this address accesses the Gate Hacking menu. When this occurs, input two Virus Core Ms into the empty slots to fill the gauge and open the area.

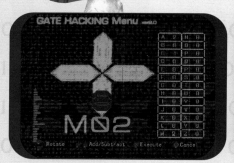

△: CLOSED, OBLIVIOUS, TWIN HILLS

REQUIRED PARTY: KITE, MIA, AND ELK

AREA VITALS	
BATTLE LEVEL:	10
ELEMENT:	Wood
GRUNTY FOOD:	Mandragora Immature Egg
ENVIRONMENT:	Grassland
WEATHER:	Night

MONSTERS
FIELD:
Mummy Ripper: Wood
Mimic
Red Wyrm: Fire
DUNGEON:
Scorpion Tank: Water
Red Wyrm: Fire

ITEMS
Leafblight
Hunter's Hood
The Fool
Defense Sword
Virus Core C
Virus Core A
Cougar Bandana
Gale Breath
Hiking Gear
Hands of Earth
Mountain Helm
Antidote

GOTT STATUE ITEMS
Fishing Gloves
Yellow Candy
Grunt Doll

RAISING
A GRUNTY

ADDITIONAL
ELEMENTS

TRADE
LIST

BOOKS
OF RYU

BESTIARY

Although there are three members in the party, the journey across this Protected Area is more difficult than any recent solo adventures. This is primarily due to Mia and Elk's low HP, but it's also because of the Mimic enemy's confusion effects. Mimics resemble Treasures but they are in fact powerful monsters with spider-like legs and a nasty bite. They often leave their prey so confused that they attack their own allies. When this occurs quickly issue a Restorative potion to the confused party member before the cursed inadvertently massacres the other party members.

Since Mia is unlikely to have any recovery skills, you can assign one of the party members the "First Aid!" command and still have a partner in physical combat. Elk will hang back and cast Repth from a safe distance to keep the group healthy, while Mia will rush the enemy and attack with her sword.

Mimics aren't the only dangerous creatures on the field in this area. The party will also run into a Red Wyrm on occasion. Use a Burning Oil to increase the group's Fire rating and continue to attack like normal. The Red Wyrm's flame attack can deliver a fair amount of damage to Mia, so make sure Elk concentrates on recovery. The group only needs to destroy a couple of Red Wyrms to gain enough EXP for Mia and Elk to level up.

COMMANDING FROM THE GRAVE

Kite may not have the ability to access his skills or items after being dealt a fatal blow, however, he can still issue Chat Commands. If Kite falls in battle, give the "First Aid!" command as quickly as possible so the other party members have time to use a Resurrect before they perish.

Dungeon, B1

Once inside the dungeon, the group is faced with an entirely different creature—the Scorpion Tank. This creature is one of the most intimidating looking monsters in "The World," but surprisingly falls rather easily with two Fire-based skill attacks. Give the group the "Skills!" command and watch the fireworks begin!

Dungeon, B2

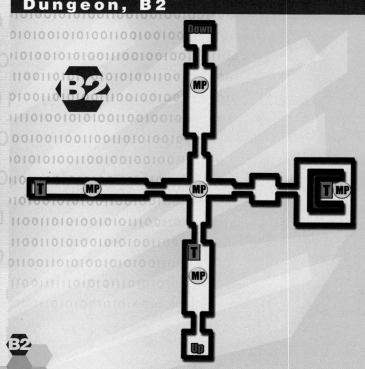

There are more Mimics and another Scorpion Tank on the second floor. Travel through the western corridor to find a Risky Treasure and an **Immature Egg**. In contrast, a Red Wyrm protects the Treasure in the room to the east. Be extra careful when taking on this particular enemy, as the tight confines of the room puts the entire party in danger of being attacked.

Dungeon, B3

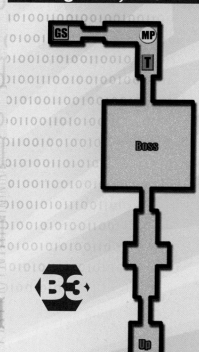

Top off everyone's HP and SP and use some of the spell scrolls (such as Knight's Blood and Hermit Blood) to raise the physical and magic attack ratings of the party members. Also, utilize the Well Water to increase each character's Earth rating. Once inside the room with the boss creature's Magic Portal, Mia instructs Kite on the importance of using the Data Drain to collect Virus Cores. Charge toward the portal to initiate the battle.

BOSS BATTLE: STONE TURTLE

level	13	**pp**	1090
hp	Infinite/1090	**sp**	800
element	Earth, counter with Wood		
skills	Rig Saem		
reward	Virus Core N		

The Stone Turtle is an extremely large conglomerate of boulders that can whirl around in a frenzy and deliver over 100 HP of damage to anyone it touches. The most difficult part of this battle is delivering enough damage to the Stone Turtle to make it susceptible to the Data Drain. To do so, give the "Skills!" command as soon as the battle begins so that everyone can get in one or two good shots. When the party members begin taking damage, order the "First Aid!" command and only switch back to the former strategy if everyone's HP is at its maximum.

Kite and Mia can deliver a large amount of damage to the Stone Turtle from traditional weapons-based attacks and through Physical Skills. Also, utilize any Wood-based scrolls, as they will score an Elemental Hit and inflict double-damage. If Kite runs low on HP, quickly back away to avoid the Stone Turtle's hefty feet and use a Health Drink to recover.

After Kite performs the Data Drain, the Stone Turtle may start using recovery spells to replenish its own lost HP. This is Kite and Mia's cue to kick up the heat and unleash a barrage of attacks. Alternate back and forth between the "Skills!" and "First Aid" commands to work Elk into the attacking strategy. When the beast reaches approximately 420 HP, perform a second Data Drain. Finish off the Stone Turtle with the powers of the bracelet to collect the **Razor Axe**.

After the boss fight, Kite explains to Mia and Elk the truth about Orca, the bracelet, and all that has transpired since Kite first logged onto "The World." Mia explains to Kite that she's interested in the bracelet purely for her own reasons, then exits back to Root Town. Kite and Elk do the same.

Now that Kite has hacked his first gate and defeated the boss lurking in the bottom of the dungeon, he is ready to move on to the more difficult areas, including those on the Θ Server. Head to the Recorder and save your game, then exit the game environment to read all of the latest postings on the Board and check your email. This is also a great time to return to the last two areas visited to clear the dungeon of its portals and collect the items from the Gott Statues that were beyond the last two bosses!

COME AGAIN?

This is another area that Kite must return to if he wants to clear the dungeon of its Magic Portals and gain the items at the Gott Statue. Consider re-entering this area immediately after defeating the boss and saving; the **Fishing Gloves** available at the Gott Statue are a very valuable piece of armor!

THE SPIRAL EDGE

The Board was quite active while Kite was off hacking the gate to the Protected Area. Read all of the new posts to see what the other players are saying about the new Neuro Goggles and Net Box. More importantly, there are some new keywords to use. Read the following posts to add the keywords to the Word List.

Thread: Let's Play Tag
Post: I'll take you on gob
Author: Jonue

0011001100110101010101010101010011001001

Ladies and Gentlegob!
Stehoney got defeated by some no name gob.
If you know what I'm talking about, come to Δ: Detestable, Golden, Messenger alone gob.
Jonue the Gobbler, one of the Four Gob Kings will take you on gob!!

Thread: Weapon Information
Post: RE: Spiral Edge
Author: Sister Ken

0011001100110101010101010101010011001001

Spiral Edge is at Δ: Raging, Passionate, Melody. But the monster there is pretty strong!

After reading the posts on the Board, exit to the desktop and check for updates in the News and Email programs. Read Helba's email, because it contains helpful information concerning the Data Drain and collecting Virus Cores from normal monsters, as well as Data Bugs. (Refer to the "Advanced Hacking" chapter for more information on this subject.) When you're finished, log back into the "The World."

Balmung is waiting in Aqua Capital Mac Anu for Kite to show up. He has come to terms with the fact that Kite is Orca's friend and Kite, in return, explains everything that has transpired thus far. However, as soon as Balmung walks away Helba appears. She is quite an enigma and riddles her way through most conversations. She warns Kite to beware of Lios and hands him **Virus Core O**. Helba departs just as suddenly as she arrived and leaves Kite with more questions than answers.

This is a good time to go after the Gob King and compete in the second round of tag (see the "Side Quests" chapter for more information on Goblin Tag). Kite has another address at his disposal—the one to the Spiral Edge. Stock up on supplies, save your game at the Recorder, and assemble a party to go after the hard-to-get weapon. It's best to spend an equal amount of time with each person who gives Kite a flash mail address. This not only enables them to level up faster, but it also increases their affection toward Kite.

For the upcoming journey, invite Piros and Mistral to the party. Trade with Mistral to receive the Bronze Axe, then give it, along with any other axes in Kite's inventory, to Piros.

AFFECTION-CHECKER

Depending on how often Kite has used the Data Drain skill so far, he may or may not have unlocked **Ryu Book V**. This book contains information on Kite's friends, including their affection. The rating can be as low as 0, or as high as 250. It's based on Kite's replies to their emails, the amount of time he spends with them, and the value of the items he gives them. Invite those party members with the lowest affection rating when given the option.

△: RAGING, PASSIONATE, MELODY

RECOMMENDED PARTY: KITE, PIROS, AND MISTRAL

AREA VITALS	
BATTLE LEVEL:	7
ELEMENT:	Fire
GRUNTY FOOD:	Grunt Mint
	Invisible Egg
ENVIRONMENT:	Molten
WEATHER:	Stormy

MONSTERS
FIELD:
Bee Army
Hob Goblin: Earth
Fiend Menhir: Thunder
DUNGEON:
Hob Goblin: Earth
Dust Curse
Bee Army
Shield Man: Darkness
Rock Head: Earth

ITEMS	
Grand Armor	Fire Tempest
The Devil	The Fool
Wind Axe	Meteor Swarm
Virus Core B	Health Drink
Meteor Swarm	Restorative
Hands of Earth	Burning Oil
Wyrm Hide	Mountain Guard

GOTT STATUE ITEMS
Spiral Edge
Grunt Doll
Rainbow Card

The enemies here are the same ones faced in previous areas. This time, however, the entire party is strong enough to dispatch the monsters with ease. Give the group the "Skills!" command and run into the center of each enemy group and unleash the powerful Tiger Claw skill. Utilize a Burning Oil to increase everyone's Fire rating, and use the symbols to gain added buffs. Thanks to the extra strength of the Bronze Axe in Piros's inventory, he can tear through Fiend Menhirs before they get a chance to resurrect fallen enemies.

The group isn't completely free of danger, however. Have plenty of Antidotes on hand; use one whenever a party member gets hit by a poisonous stinger from the Bee Armies. If left untreated, these toxins will slowly diminish the HP of the infected, thus leading to a premature death!

Dungeon, B1

The party finds a terrified Natsume just inside the entrance to the dungeon. She wanted the Spiral Edge, but got scared when she encountered monsters in the dungeon. Perhaps Kite can retrieve the weapon for her? Leave Natsume in the entrance room and continue into the dungeon.

The monsters inside this dungeon are the same as those in the field, the lone exception being the Shield Man. Explore the dungeon's corners to collect all of the various treasure and **Invisible Eggs**. Continue to use the same tactics previously used in the field to deal with the monsters at each Magic Portal.

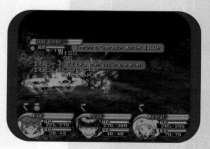

Dungeon, B2

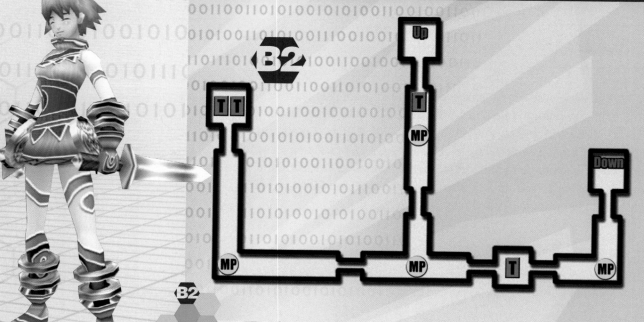

Dungeon, B3

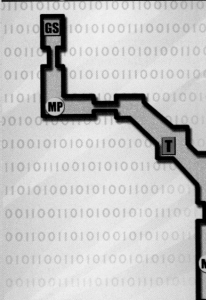

Kite and Piros face a tougher battle on the third floor when they encounter a Rock Head. Issue the "Skills!" command again, but watch everyone's HP levels closely. The Rock Head's whirling boulders can inflict lots of damage in a short period of time. If possible, use a Wood-based skill or item (such as Green Gale) to score an Elemental Hit.

After grabbing the **Spiral Edge** from the Gott Statue, Natsume appears and asks for it. This is a bit of a dilemma for Kite, as the Spiral Edge is a weapon for those in the Twin Blade class. Nevertheless, Natsume will give Kite her flash address if he gives her the weapon. Hand her the Spiral Edge, then return to Root Town.

SPOTTED AGAIN!

Exit Aqua Capital Mac Anu and check the Board for new posts. Read each thread with a new post to gain new keyword addresses. Most importantly, read the one that mentions seeing the mysterious girl on the Θ server.

✉ **Thread: Is This an Event Character**　　**Author: Marin**
Post: RE: Girl

Marin saw her too.

Girl in a white dress was chased by a thing with a red wand.

Θ: Quiet, Eternal, White Devil

... I think.

... But I can't enter it any more, why?

After reading the postings on the Board, return to the desktop and check Kite's email for new messages. One of them is scrambled into a barely decipherable mess. Although much of the text is scrambled in a manner similar to that of the Data Bugs, the line "Bearer of the bracelet, help me before there are any more casualties" is identifiable. Could this be another email from the girl?

There's even a message from BlackRose. In it, she repeats the address posted on the Board. She'd like to meet Kite on the Θ server to investigate. After reading her email, access to the Θ server becomes available.

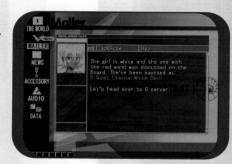

✉ **Thread: BlackRose**
Subject: Hey

The girl in white and the one with the red wand was discussed on the Board. They've been spotted at Θ: Quiet, Eternal, White Devil.

Let's head over to Θ server.

Log back into "The World" and approach the Chaos Gate on Δ server. Select Θ server from the "Other Servers" option to warp to Highland City Dun Loireag, the Root Town of the other server. BlackRose is waiting there and tells Kite to meet her back at the Chaos Gate as soon as possible.

Take the opportunity to wander around this new town. Highland City Dun Loireag has the same shops as Aqua Capital Mac Anu, but the available items are more powerful. Also, Kite is more likely to encounter advanced players on the θ server, so higher-stakes trades are more common.

The best feature of this new town is the Grunty Ranch. When ready to assume the role of "dad," Kite can adopt a Little Grunty and raise it into an intelligent adult. You can ride adult Grunties in the field to decrease travel time over great distances but, more importantly, you can trade some Grunties for rare and powerful items. Refer to the "Raising a Grunty" chapter for more tips on raising these helpful creatures.

SAFE HAVEN

Don't worry about leaving behind valuable items and weaponry at the Elf's Haven in Aqua Capital Mac Anu. Each of the Elf's Havens is connected, so Kite can access his stored items in any Root Town.

θ: QUIET, ETERNAL, WHITE DEVIL

RECOMMENDED PARTY: KITE, BLACKROSE, AND NATSUME

AREA VITALS		MONSTERS	ITEMS		GOTT STATUE ITEMS
BATTLE LEVEL:	13	FIELD:	Virus Core C	Antidote	The Gott Statue is unreachable at this time.
ELEMENT:	Water	Mimic	Hands of Earth	Wyrm Scale	
		Cyclo Shark: Water	Snow Panther	The Lovers	
GRUNTY FOOD:	Cordyceps	DUNGEON:	The Hanged Man	Frost Armor	
	Bear Cat Egg	Cyclo Shark: Water	Ice Storm	Restorative	
	Golden Egg	Hungry Grass: Wood	Ice Floe	Health Drink	
		Thousand Trees: Wood	The Death	Frost Bracer	
ENVIRONMENT:	Snowfield	Guardian: Earth	Shadow Blades	Raccoon Earcap	
		Crab Turtle: Water	Pure Water	The Moon	
WEATHER:	Snowing				

Since Natsume is a Level 1 Twin Blade, it's important to keep a close eye on her during battles. However, she's going to level up quickly and can even reach Level 6 before the group enters the dungeon! To make things easier, give her every lightweight piece of armor and spare Twin Blade weapon in Kite's inventory. Although Natsume has the Spiral Edge weapon, giving her other weapons will help raise her affection for the group's leader from its current low level.

There are two types of monsters in this field: the Mimics and the Cyclo Sharks. Although the Cyclo Shark is much larger and packs more HP, it's actually easier to defeat. Have the group utilize Fire-based skills and items, then have Kite attack the creature up close with the Flame Dance physical attack skill (if it's still equipped). The group can dish out even more

damage to the Cyclo Shark by utilizing a Burning Oil to increase their Fire rating. Similarly, use Pure Water to increase the party's Water rating to reduce the damage received from the beast. Lastly, never run from a Cyclo Shark! Although it looks ferocious, Natsume gains nearly 500 EXP for each slain creature when she is at her early levels.

SPOTTED AGAIN!

IN A CONFUSED STATE

When a party member becomes Confused, he or she may attack his or her allies. Although this isn't bad if Natsume starts to attack Kite or BlackRose, it could have devastating effects on the success of the group if Kite should suffer the consequences of the spell. Carry lots of Resurrects and Restoratives and divide them up between the party members in case one of the stronger characters goes on an uncontrollable killing spree. Even when dead, Kite can issue the "First Aid!" command in hopes of having an ally Resurrect his fallen body.

Mimics, on the other hand, attack in groups of two to four and have the ability to Confuse their prey. They are also quite resilient and can take lots of damage before succumbing to physical attacks. Have Kite and BlackRose act as the lead attackers against the Mimics and, for the time being, give Natsume the "Standby" command to keep her out of harm's way. When the yellow Confusion icon appears next to a party member's status bar, administer a Restorative to cure the ailment. If Natsume falls in battle with a Mimic, Resurrect her before slaying the beast. Remember, she can gain over 200 EXP from each Mimic early in the adventure.

One of the best features of this particular field area is the abundance of Symbols. Keep a lookout for solitary flames on the horizon and take advantage of these spell-casting torches whenever possible. In contrast, there isn't much Grunty Food available. Although Kite may encounter an occasional Cordyceps poking through the snow, they aren't easy to spot.

Dungeon, B1

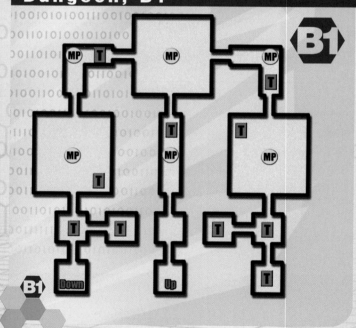

The dungeon contains numerous Cyclo Sharks and they seem to behave much more aggressively here than they did on the field. Avoid their tail attack and stay back as far as possible when attacking.

Several of the rooms on this floor are quite large and may contain a **Bear Cat** or **Golden Egg** in the corner. Also, smash each of the Warrior's Bodies in hopes of gaining a Restorative. You can never have too many when fighting Mimics!

There are two new Wood-based enemies in the halls of the dungeon: the Hungry Grass and the Thousand Trees. The Hungry Grass doesn't inflict much damage, but it does put its prey to Sleep…yet another reason to hoard Restoratives. The Thousand Trees, with 1090 HP, has the ability to cast spells against the group. Use Earth-based items or skills against it. The Raging Earth and Raining Rocks scrolls work especially well against this beast.

Travel to the southeastern corner of this dungeon and collect the items from the Treasures. Although the Ice Floes and Ice Storm scrolls aren't all that helpful in this dungeon, they will come in handy later when traveling to areas with more Fire-based creatures.

RAISING
A GRUNTY

ADDITIONAL
ELEMENTS

TRADE
LIST

BOOKS
OF RYU

BESTIARY

Dungeon, B2

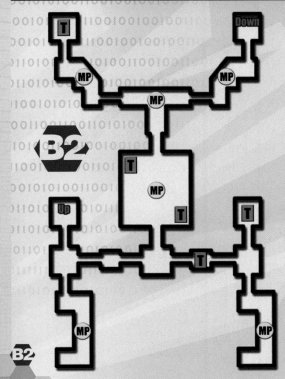

The second floor of the dungeon is home to some rather large creatures, like the Thousand Trees and the Guardian. The Guardian is an Earth-based monster that walks on two enormous stone pillars and uses them to stomp on its adversaries. Issue the "Skills!" command and utilize the Tiger Claws unless Kite is equipped with the Oak Anklet. This will allow for some Elemental Hits via its accompanying skills.

Exercise caution when entering the room in the northwestern corner. The Magic Portal in here contains a pair of Guardians and a Hungry Grass enemy. Command BlackRose to attack the Hungry Grass immediately to avoid having the party put to sleep with the two enormous Guardians walking around. Once the Hungry Grass is defeated, give the "First Aid!" command to have the three attack with their weapons, but also monitor everyone's health.

Dungeon, B3

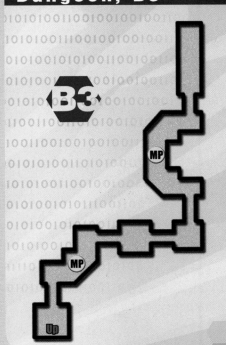

Battle through the monsters in the first few rooms to clear the dungeon of all of its Magic Portals, then continue on to what appears to be a dead end. Although there's something obviously wrong, there's nothing to do right now. Return to Root Town, save your game at the Recorder, and log out of "The World" to check email and the Board.

SPOTTED AGAIN!

ELK'S JEALOUSY

Elk
Mia, you've been acting weird lately. Why do you care about that guy so much?

Elk
Mia, uh – uh... I... I like you.

Since Kite doesn't have access to any more keywords and both the Board and his email inbox are showing little signs of life, see what's going over on the Δ server. While warping to Aqua Capital Mac Anu, Elk confronts Mia about the newcomer with the bracelet. Elk is clearly jealous of Mia's new friendship with Kite and tells Mia that he likes her.

Elk is standing near the Chaos Gate when Kite arrives in Root Town and asks Kite to help him fix one of his favorite areas. Elk thinks the area may have become infected with a Data Bug. The area is **Δ: Plenteous, Smiling, Hypha**. Head over to the Recorder to save your game, then wander around town to trade for items that will benefit the young Wavemaster. Trade with Henako or A-Kichi for the Cedar Wand. Return to the Chaos Gate, have Elk join the party, and head off to the area he selected.

Elk
You're the only one who can help. The area is Λ Plenteous Smiling Hypha. Can you come with me?

Δ: PLENTEOUS, SMILING, HYPHA
REQUIRED PARTY: KITE AND ELK

AREA VITALS	
BATTLE LEVEL:	14
ELEMENT:	Wood
GRUNTY FOOD:	Mushroom
	Invisible Egg
ENVIRONMENT:	Mountains
WEATHER:	Cloudy

MONSTERS
FIELD:
Heavy Metal: Thunder
Hungry Grass: Wood
Thousand Trees: Wood
DUNGEON:
Water Witch: Water
Heavy Metal: Thunder
Thousand Trees: Wood

ITEMS	
Mountain Boots	Ronin Blades
Frost Bracer	Spark Blades
Mountain Boots	Flame Axe
Mountain Guard	Antidote
Cougar Bandana	Holy Sap
Spark Blades	Restorative
Gale Breath	Virus Core A
Green Gale	The Fool
The Devil	

GOTT STATUE ITEMS
Firedrake Mail
Rainbow Card
Rainbow Card

Elk
I'll give you every item I have. In return for – um... Can you give me your bracelet?

It takes only a few moments for Kite to realize that there's nothing wrong with this area; Elk brought him here for other reasons. Elk meekly asks for Kite's bracelet in exchange for every item in Elk's possession. Elk wants the bracelet so Mia will hang out with him again. Just as Elk finishes explaining his motives, a large shadow sweeps over them and the area begins to become infected.

RAISING
A GRUNTY

ADDITIONAL
ELEMENTS

TRADE
LIST

BOOKS
OF RYU

BESTIARY

Whether or not the enemies in the field pose a serious threat depends on the duo's levels. Kite's level should be fine, but Elk could possibly be as low as Level 9 (that is if he hasn't been in Kite's party much). Give any weapons and armor to Elk that boost his physical and magical ratings and keep an eye on him in battle.

The familiar Thousand Trees and Hungry Grass enemiesabound in the field, as well as the Thunder-based Heavy Metal unit. These axe-wielding soldiers attack in groups and are quite resilient. Beat them down with physical skill attacks, such as the Tiger Claws, then use the Data Drain to retrieve the **Ronin Blades** from them. Because of the abundance of Wood-based enemies in the area, don't equip the Ronin Blades just yet. Make sure you hold onto them for later, though.

The field is loaded with Symbols and Mushrooms and it even contains a Spring of Myst. The conditions are right and Monsieur is feeling helpful today; toss in a weapon, let him know that it was neither a Golden Axe nor Silver Axe, and sit back and watch as he turns it into a better piece of equipment.

Dungeon, B1

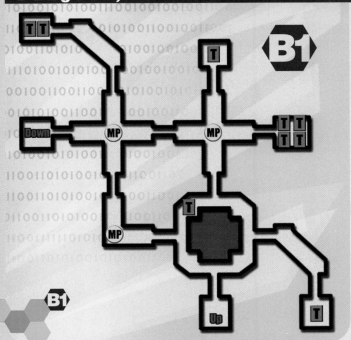

As the pair enters the dungeon, it becomes clear the area has definitely become infected with the virus. Elk's lie has come true… but why?

0111001001010101011101011010

ITEM LIMITS

Kite may run out of inventory room while in this area. Although he can always swap out one item for another, it's best to give any unwanted items to Elk instead of discarding them altogether. Even items unusable to Elk will help raise his affection toward Kite.

The party is likely to encounter a new enemy known as the Water Witch en route to the treasure room to the northeast. Water Witches have very low HP and are susceptible to a Fire-based skill or scroll, as well as any physical attack. Continue the trek to the northeastern room and collect the contents of the Treasures and urns there. Hold onto any Gale Breath scrolls you come across, because they will come in handy during the upcoming boss fight.

Dungeon, B2

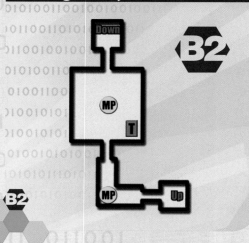

Dungeon, B3

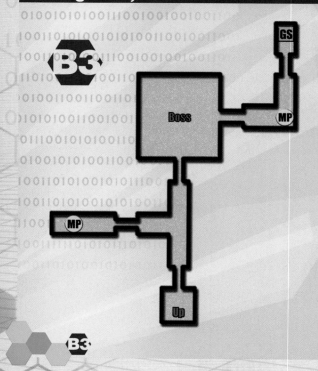

Before walking through the purple light, take a moment to prepare for the boss fight. The Killer Snaker is an Earth-based creature, so attack it with Wood-based skills and scrolls. Equip the Ronin Blades and make sure Elk has the Cedar Wand ready to go. Also, divvy up the Green Gales and Gale Breath scrolls and use a Holy Sap to increase the duo's Wood rating. Make the most of additional strengthening items such as Knight's Blood, Hermit Blood, or Beast Blood.

BOSS BATTLE: KILLER SNAKER

level	16	**pp**	485
hp	20,208/1330	**sp**	970
element	Earth, counter with Wood		
skills	MeGan Rom		
reward	Virus Core P		

Kite and Elk find Mia alone in the large room next to the Magic Portal. She calls out to Elk and he and Kite rush to her rescue. Mia joins the two in battle against the Data Bug, although she will remain out of Kite's control.

Thanks to the Ronin Blades (acquired by Data Draining the Heavy Metals), Kite has an incredibly powerful physical attack skill called the Gale of Swords. Get in close to the beast and unleash this amazing attack. It can almost single-handedly reduce the Data Bug to a point where it can be Data Drained. If possible, use a Mage's Soul to replenish Kite's SP and use the attack again.

Stand back out of harm's reach and issue the "First Aid!" command to Elk. While Elk acts as a healer, Kite can cast spell after spell to continually diminish the Killer Snaker's HP.

You can Data Drain the Killer Snaker a second time once its HP falls below 400. Doing so at that point will put a speedy end to the battle. A very valuable **Fire Lizard** item is the reward for winning this battle.

After the boss fight, Mia explains to Elk that she was looking for him…that she misses him. After discussing the loss of their favorite area, the two warp back to Root Town. Kite follows soon after.

Mia
I'm not sure, but - I miss you when you're not around.

COME AGAIN?

Kite must make a second trip through this dungeon to collect the items at the Gott Statue. Invite Mistral and Natsume to join Kite in a quick revisit to the dungeon. Clear out the Magic Portals and claim the items at the Gott Statue right after returning to Root Town.

THE KOTETSU SWORD

Kite discovers that many players had posted keywords to different areas on the Board while Elk was leading him on a wild goose chase. Read the following posts to record the keywords, then return to Aqua Capital Mac Anu.

Thread: Let's Play Tag   **Author: Zyan**
Post: Is it my turn?

Didn't think you'd get this far gob. Sorry, sorry, I was thinking you guys were stupid gob.

But now that I'm here, it won't be that easy gob. Eavesdropping Zyan, one of the Four Gob Kings will be waiting at Δ: Detestable, Golden, Scent gob.

Come along gob!

Thread: Weapon Information   **Author: unyu**
Post: then

If you're level 8, I recommend the "Kotetsu Sword" in Δ: Hideous, Destroyer's, Far Thunder.

Thread: Miss Gardenia Fan Club!!   **Author: Moeri**
Post: RE: Just a loser

Miss Gardenia's favorite area these days is Θ: Soft, Solitary, Tri Pansy.

Why don't we get together? We might be able to meet Miss Gardenia!

BY THE NUMBERS

Piros's struggle may seem urgent, but the big lug is patient and will wait for Kite to assist him at the Twin Blade's earliest convenience. Although you can complete these quests in any order, the area where the Kotetsu Sword is rumored to be is a Level 12 area. On the other hand, the one with Piros's cure is a Level 16 area. The party members will gain more EXP in the long run by attacking the lower level first.

Kite arrives back in Root Town in time to see Mia give Piros a mysterious item that turns Piros orange. It's thought to be a magic love potion and can only be cured by finding the remedy in Δ: **Putrid, Hot-Blooded, Scaffold**. Piros wants Kite to join him on his quest to find the remedy. Go to the Chaos Gate and invite Piros to join your party.

Rather than head off with Piros, meet the next Goblin King for the next round of Goblin Tag. After doing so, head off in search of the Kotetsu Sword with Natsume and Mistral.

△: HIDEOUS, DESTROYER'S, FAR THUNDER

RECOMMENDED PARTY: KITE, NATSUME, AND MISTRAL

AREA VITALS

BATTLE LEVEL:	12
ELEMENT:	Fire
GRUNTY FOOD:	Twilight Onion
	Bear Cat Egg
ENVIRONMENT:	Molten
WEATHER:	Very Hot

MONSTERS

FIELD:
Hungry Grass: Wood
Guardian: Earth
Mimic

DUNGEON:
Guardian: Earth
Red Wyrm: Fire
Thousand Trees: Wood

ITEMS

Razor Axe	Restorative
Ceramic Anklet	Meteor Swarm
The Death	Fire Tempest
Hands of Earth	The Lovers
Assasin	Health Drink
The Hanged Man	Stun Sword
Antidote	The Moon

GOTT STATUE ITEMS

Kotetsu Sword
Yellow Candy
Grunt Doll

If you've been thorough during the previous quests and cleared each area's Magic Portals, Kite should be near a Level 13 Twin Blade or perhaps even higher. Although there is very little EXP to gain for slaying the beasts on this level, it's a good idea to sweep the field clean of monsters to help Natsume and Mistral gain their own EXP.

The enemies in this particular field should all look familiar. Use the Ronin Blades to unleash the Gale of Swords attack on the Guardian enemies. Also, bring plenty of Restoratives to cure Confusion caused by the Mimics.

Dungeon, B1

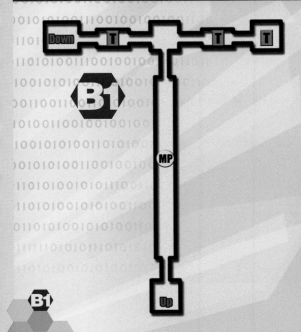

Kite and his traveling partners run into a player named Sanjuro inside the entrance to the dungeon. Sanjuro can't find the Kotetsu Sword. Step past Sanjuro and into the next room of the dungeon. If the Kotetsu Sword is here, Kite's bound to find it!

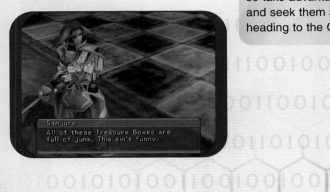

A REPRIEVE OF SORTS

The layout of this dungeon is very straightforward, which makes navigation much simpler. There are very few Magic Portals in the entire dungeon, so take advantage of that fact and seek them all out before heading to the Gott Statue.

Dungeon, B2

There is a Red Wyrm guarding the path to the staircase leading to the dungeon's lowest level. Back away from the beast's tail and use Ice Floe and Ice Storm scrolls to inflict Elemental Hits on it. Issue the "Skills!" command so the other party members can make the most of what they have.

Dungeon, B3

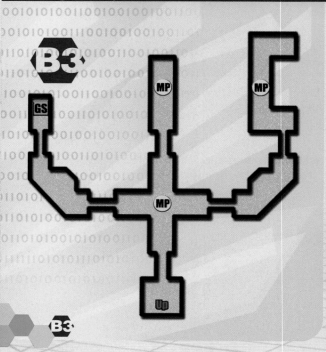

Destroy the Red Wyrm blocking the central intersection, then explore the east and north routes before heading to the west to clear the dungeon of its Magic Portals. After sweeping the area clean, head to the west and open the Treasure at the Gott Statue to take possession of the **Kotetsu Sword**.

Kite returns to Sanjuro near the dungeon's entrance and informs Sanjuro that he found the sword. Like Natsume before him, Sanjuro asks for the weapon. Give the Kotetsu Sword to Sanjuro in exchange for his flash mail address and the Tolerance Book.

MAGIC LOVE POTION

Piros has waited long enough; it's time to join him on his quest to find a cure to the magical potion Mia infected him with. Invite Piros and Sanjuro to join the party. Give any Heavy Blade weapons or unusable armor to Sanjuro to increase his affection toward Kite.

NO GIFTS FOR PIROS

Kite can't trade or give items to Piros until he is cured of his malady.

△: PUTRID, HOT-BLOODED, SCAFFOLD

RECOMMENDED PARTY: KITE, PIROS, AND SANJURO

AREA VITALS

BATTLE LEVEL:	16
ELEMENT:	Wood
GRUNTY FOOD:	Mushroom
	Invisible Egg
	Golden Egg
ENVIRONMENT:	Mountains
WEATHER:	Partly Cloudy

MONSTERS

FIELD:
Shining Eyes: Darkness
Nomadic Bones: Darkness
Squilla Demon: Water

DUNGEON:
Nomadic Bones: Darkness
Squilla Demon: Water
Sled Dog: Fire
Goblin Wiz: Fire

ITEMS

Gale Breath	Holy Sap
Virus Core B	Health Drink
Diabolic Wand	Restorative
Spear of Spell	Antidote
The Fool	Hands of Earth
Ceramic Anklet	Miner's Gloves
The Death	Aqua Guard
Frost Anklet	Mountain Guard
Green Gale	Healing Potion
The Devil	Wind Axe

GOTT STATUE ITEMS

Firedrake Mail
Rainbow Card
Rainbow Card

Sanjuro is already at Level 15, which makes him a great partner for this area. The field contains two Darkness-based enemies and another enemy aligned with Water. Equip Kite with items that enable Thunder- and Fire-based attacks.

Since Kite probably has several Fire-based magical attack spells, dealing with the Squilla Demon shouldn't prove too difficult. Additionally, a series of normal attacks can deplete the Nomadic Bones enemy of its low HP in no time. What makes the battles on this level difficult is the presence of the Shining Eyes enemy. These large, floating spirits twirl a sharp sword and unleash the blade upon their prey with ferocious speed. Equip Piros with the Thunder Axe, provided it was given to him earlier. Issue the "Skills!" command so Piros can strike the Shining Eyes with an Elemental Hit.

Kite, Piros, and Sanjuro may make for a powerful party, but they lack a reliable spell-caster. Give the group the "Skills!" command and allow Piros and Sanjuro to lead the attack against the Shining Eyes while Kite hangs back and casts La Repth or doles out Health Drinks. Of course, if Kite can attack with a Thunder-based skill, then let him join the fight.

Dungeon, B1

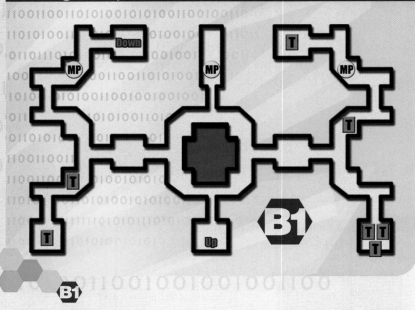

The dungeon in this area is quite large and contains lots of monsters and Treasures. Each of the four floors in the dungeon contains a possible remedy for Piros, but only the one on the fourth floor will successfully cure him. The others simply turn him different colors. The first Remedy is in the southeastern corner of this floor.

In addition to the Treasures and remedies, there are numerous **Invisible Eggs** and **Golden Eggs** to find. Explore each room to collect these hard-to-find types of food.

Dungeon, B2

The second floor is very unique in that it doesn't contain any Magic Portals. Lead the party to the northwest corner of the dungeon to find the **Custom Remedy**.

Dungeon, B3

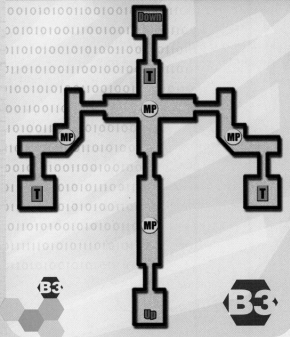

The party encounters two new enemies on the third floor of the dungeon. The Sled Dog and Goblin Wiz are both aligned with the Fire element, thus making them susceptible to damage from the Ice Floe and Ice Storm scrolls. Use Pure Water to increase the party's Water rating, and issue the "Skills!" command when encountering these baddies in battle.

The staircase leading down to the fourth and final floor is directly north of the staircase leading back upstairs. Nevertheless, gain extra EXP and items by exploring the east and west wings of the floor. Piros can give the **True Remedy** a try by taking it from the Treasure in the southwest corner of the floor.

Dungeon, B4

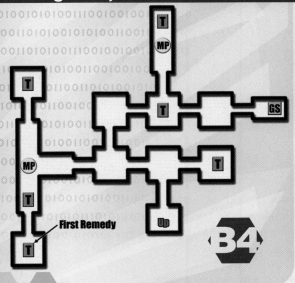

First Remedy

The lowest level in this dungeon contains lots of items, Treasures, and Golden Eggs. It also contains a Gott Statue and the cure to Piros's ailments…the **First Remedy**. Travel to the northeast corner of the dungeon to collect the items from the Gott Statue before seeking the First Remedy in the southwest corner. Once Piros is cured, the group automatically returns to Root Town.

MAKE ROOM FOR THE POTIONS

You will most likely acquire several Health Potions from Treasures and breakable objects on this floor of the dungeon. Health Potions are much more potent than Health Drinks, so hold onto them until the party members have at least 400 HP and can take full advantage of a Health Potion's powers.

Once cured, Piros gives Kite his diary. **Piros's Diary** appears under the "Books" heading on the Items Menu screen. Unfortunately, the item actually takes away from the user's Magical Attack rating. Once back in Root Town, store Piros's Diary at the Elf's Haven to free up a valuable inventory slot.

MISS GARDENIA'S LETTER

It's apparent from reading the messages on the Board that the player by the name of Miss Gardenia has a very strong following. An earlier post suggested that a group of girls were going to meet at an area on the Θ server. Warp to the other server and find out what all the fuss is about.

Θ: SOFT, SOLITARY, TRI PANSY

RECOMMENDED PARTY: KITE, SANJURO, AND NATSUME

AREA VITALS

BATTLE LEVEL: 14
ELEMENT: Wood
GRUNTY FOOD: Piney Apple
Invisible Egg
Golden Egg
ENVIRONMENT: Jungle
WEATHER: Sunny

MONSTERS

FIELD:
Thousand Trees: Wood
Heavy Metal: Thunder
Water Witch: Water
DUNGEON:
Heavy Metal: Thunder
Water Witch: Water
Hungry Grass: Wood
Menhir: Thunder
Guardian: Earth

ITEMS

Green Gale
The Fool
Gale Breath
Virus Core C
Wyrm Scale
The Devil
Holy Sap
Antidote
Restorative
Ronin Blades
Health Drink
Virus Core A
Frost Armor
The Death
Earth Axe

GOTT STATUE ITEMS

Bloody Blades
Silver Scarab
Yellow Candy

Field

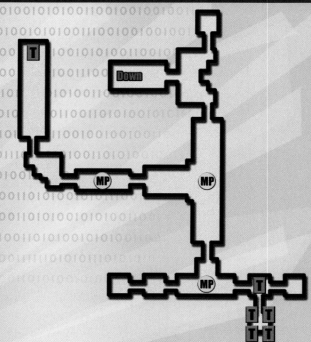

FIELD MAP

This is the first visit to a jungle area and, this may come as a surprise, but the fields in these areas have well-defined boundaries not unlike the dungeons. You can quickly clear these areas of Magic Portals; don't let the opportunity pass!

Having just completed a quest at a Level 16 area, this particular adventure should be relatively easy. There are only three Magic Portals and they contain monsters that Kite has seen numerous times before.

Search the southern portion of the field thoroughly and collect as many **Piney Apples** as possible. Piney Apples are restricted to the jungle areas and are among the rarest of all Grunty Food!

Dungeon, B1

Once inside the dungeon, a player named Heril asks Kite to deliver a love letter to Miss Gardenia. Heril and her friends are huge fans of Miss Gardenia, but they're too weak to follow her into the depths of the dungeon. Kite begrudgingly accepts the mission and heads off in search of the mystery woman.

The uppermost floor of the dungeon contains just one Magic Portal, but each of the spurs leading off the central path are loaded with Treasures and **Invisible** and **Golden Eggs**. Explore the far corners of B1, then head north to the staircase leading down to the next level.

Kite encounters Miss Gardenia at the entrance to the second floor. She is all too familiar with the girls who claim to be her fans and refuses to accept the letter. She then turns and runs deeper into the dungeon, thereby leaving Kite with no option but to chase her.

Dungeon, B2

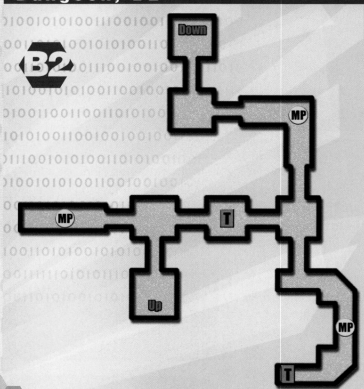

There are a couple of battles against familiar foes on B2. Issue the "Skills!" command to Natsume and Sanjuro, then use the Data Drain to finish off the monsters after inflicting substantial damage.

Miss Gardenia is waiting near the staircase once again…and once again she flees into the depths of the dungeon. The chase continues…

Dungeon, B3

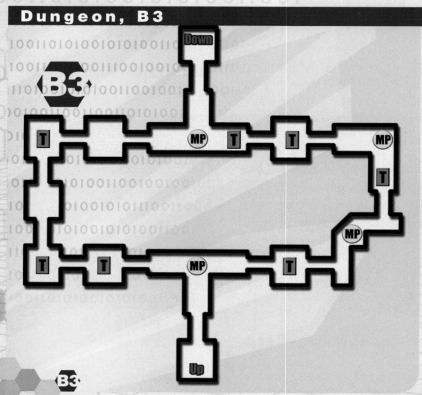

The rooms on this floor form a large circle that connects the two staircases with one another. There are many Treasures on this floor, as well as some adversaries. If a Hungry Grass enemy appears, go after it first to avoid being put to sleep. Follow Miss Gardenia into the lowest floor in the dungeon.

RAISING
A GRUNTY

ADDITIONAL
ELEMENTS

TRADE
LIST

BOOKS
OF RYU

BESTIARY

Dungeon, B4

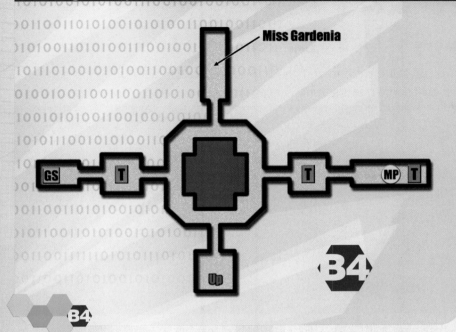

Miss Gardenia

The fourth floor in the dungeon is the smallest one of all and, while Kite may be anxious to quickly head north and track Miss Gardenia down once and for all, it's best to explore the east and west wings first. The final Magic Portal is in the eastern hallway, while the Gott Statue is to the west.

It's highly likely that an encounter with the Menhir enemy will occur on this level. This creature, a relative of the Fiend Menhir, hops around the room quite fast and can stomp its prey if they don't stay out of reach. Allow the other party members to attack the Menhir, then Data Drain it once the creature has been weakened.

Upon reaching the northernmost corridor on this floor, Kite finds Miss Gardenia struggling in a battle against a Guardian. Quickly rush to her aid and use some Green Gale and Gale Breath scrolls to aid in the fight. Miss Gardenia is impressed by Kite's strength and decides to accept the letter as long as he allows her to invite him to her party and stops calling her "miss." Gardenia gives Kite her flash mail address, then uses an item to escape the dungeon without running into her fan club.

PROTECTED AREA #2

Virus Core Requirements: 2 "A," 1 "N"

After helping Piros you're out of keywords, so exit the game and check for new email. In addition to the growing number of friendly emails, BlackRose reveals some news she has uncovered.

Sender: BlackRose
Subject: WOW!

When we went to the dungeon of ⊖: Quiet, Eternal, White Devil nothing was there, right?

I thought it was a hoax, so I e-mailed... uh... Marin was it? Well, anyways, I e-mailed her.

She wouldn't reply to me, but I kept pestering her and guess what!

Someone changed those keywords! She was freaked about it too!

The actual keywords are ⊖: Cursed, Despaired, Paradise.

You're still gonna go, right?

With a new set of keywords and a person to go exploring with, return to ⊖ server and attempt to warp to the area with BlackRose and Gardenia. As it turns out, the area is protected and Kite doesn't have the necessary Virus Core Q to hack it. This isn't such a bad thing, as the area is Level 20. Kite needs to gain some more EXP before exploring there.

It's looking more and more like someone is changing the keywords that get posted on the board. Log back out of the game and check for new email to see if anything else has come up. Kite may have several emails that appear to be friendly conversation, with one exception. Mistral is starting to wonder where Kite has been. Reply to her email letting her know to go to the ⊖ server. Exit the email program and log back into "The World."

Sender: Mistral
Subject: Hi hi!

Hellooooo.

Haven't seen you in a while, so what's up? I wanna see that cool trick again, so call me!!!

TO BE CONTINUED...

The Book of Iron is like the Book of Law in that neither of them can be used in *.hack//INFECTION*. Instead, they are designed to be carried over to subsequent volumes of the *.hack* series.

Kite finds Mistral haggling over a valuable item with Apeiron in Highland City Dun Loireag when he returns. After Mistral leaves, Apeiron not only offers the **Book of Iron** to Kite at a lower price, but ultimately forces it upon Kite after he refuses. Apeiron then warns about a notorious hacker named Helba and logs out of the game.

Shortly after Apeiron leaves, Mistral shows up. She heard of a dangerous area and wants Kite to go with her to explore it. The area is **θ: Collapsed, Momentary, Spiral**. Like the keywords BlackRose provided, this too is a Protected Area. However, Kite should have the correct Virus Cores in his possession to hack this gate.

Before venturing off into battle, do some helpful trading or "gifting" ahead of time. It's important to trade with Gardenia to acquire the **Spell Blades**. Also, if there are duplicate pieces of armor or weapons in Kite's inventory, provide some to her, particularly the Merman Spear.

WEAPONS COLLECTION

Although many of the Level 8 and 9 Twin Blades weapons contain the all-purpose Tiger Claws skill, it's time for Kite to carry multiple weapons so he can switch between their element-specific physical attacks. Hold onto the Ronin Blades (Wood), Sotetsu (Fire), Bloody Blades (Darkness), and Spell Blades (Thunder) and use them to counter elemental tolerances of the stronger enemies.

θ: COLLAPSED, MOMENTARY, SPIRAL

RECOMMENDED PARTY: KITE, MISTRAL, AND GARDENIA

AREA VITALS	
BATTLE LEVEL:	19
ELEMENT:	Earth
GRUNTY FOOD:	Rooty Vegetable Invisible Egg
ENVIRONMENT:	Grassland
WEATHER:	Night

MONSTERS
FIELD:
Dark Witch: Darkness
Noisy Wisp: Darkness
Phantom Wing
DUNGEON:
Menhir: Thunder
Phantom Wing
Dark Witch: Darkness

ITEMS	
Fire Dance Hat	Antidote
Earth Rod	Restorative
Raging Earth	Health Drink
Virus Core A	The Hanged Man
Fireman's Coat	The Death
Firedrake Mail	Raining Rocks
Fire Helm	Shanato
Blaze Armor	Well Water

GOTT STATUE ITEMS
Sotetsu
Silver Scarab (x2)

There is no getting around the fact that the enemies in this area are much tougher than previous ones. To make matters worse, Gardenia is only a Level 10 Long Arm when Kite first begins playing with her—everyone's got to start somewhere! Help the party out by giving Mistral any light armor or wands, such as the Diabolic Wand (if there's one in Kite's inventory).

Two of the three enemies on the field are aligned with Darkness, thus making the Spell Blades a very timely acquisition. Save SP by using the Tiger Claws when attacking the weaker Dark Witch, but utilize the Lightning Rage skill when fighting a Noisy Wisp. Both of these enemies attack the party with powerful Darkness skills and the longer they are allowed to live, the more likely it becomes that a party member will fall.

PROTECTED AREA #2

The third type of monster encountered on the field is the Phantom Wing. This creature isn't aligned with any specific element, yet it is difficult to slay with hand-to-hand combat due to its ability to fly. Prove the old adage that what goes up must come down, and use a Green Gale scroll to blow it out of the air!

Gardenia may perish once during the first battles, but the large disparity in levels and experience will net her large amounts of EXP for every kill someone in the party makes. Give the "First Aid!" command after someone falls below 100 HP, and rely on Mistral's healing powers to keep Kite and Gardenia alive.

Dungeon, B1

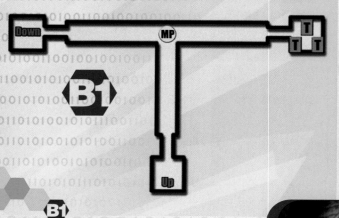

Mistral shows Kite just how naïve she is about the goings-on in "The World" by remarking on the "cool effects" added to this area's dungeon walls. Kite knows what she thinks is cool is really the virus slowly corrupting the online graphics files.

The group isn't likely to encounter any Noisy Wisps in the dungeon, but the presence of the Menhir is even more troubling. Dispose of the Menhirs first, because they have the power to heal and resurrect the other monsters. Switch to the Bloody Blades and its Twin Darkness skill to counter its Thunder tolerance.

Dungeon, B2

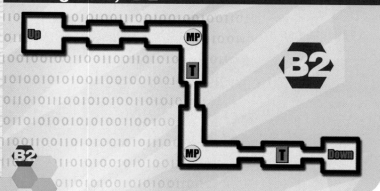

Dungeon, B3

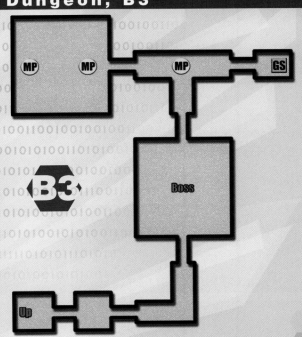

The people Mistral overheard at the weapons shop were correct—this place is dangerous! In fact, there's an infected Thousand Trees creature in the main room of this floor. It's a Data Bug, therefore it must be Data Drained to defeat it. First, however, Kite and the others must prepare for battle.

Use one of the Well Water items to raise everyone's Earth rating, then issue Knight's Blood and Beast's Blood to each of the party members individually. Equip Kite with one of the weapons other than the Ronin Blade, then proceed through the purple haze to fight the boss.

BOSS BATTLE: THOUSAND TREES

level	18	pp	2750
hp	20,234/1090	sp	185
element	Wood, counter with Earth		
skills	RaJuk Rom		
reward	Virus Core Q		

The Data Bug has a large reach with its tree branch arms and is quite impervious to physical attacks. Nevertheless, there was a reason so many crates and urns in this dungeon contained Raining Rocks and Raging Earth scrolls—use them to swiftly neutralize this enemy!

Stand a safe distance from the boss and issue the "Skills!" command to the party. While Mistral and Gardenia whittle away at the creature's HP, have Kite cast consecutive Earth-based scrolls to quickly reduce the creature to the point at which it can be Data Drained. Perform the Data Drain to obtain **Virus Core Q**.

Once the Data Bug has been squashed and the normal Thousand Trees remains, use another Raging Earth scroll to bring the arboreal monster to a point at which it can be Data Drained a second time. Let the bracelet end the fight once and for all. Now Kite has the Virus Core needed to investigate that other area!

COME AGAIN?

After the fight, turn around and return to the dungeon to clear it of Magic Portals and collect the items from the Gott Statue. Beware of the battle in the northwest corner of B3; there are numerous Menhirs and Dark Witches there. Have several Mage's Souls on hand and use the Lightning Rage skill to dispose of the Menhirs quickly. It's tough, but the extra EXP is worth it!

PROTECTED AREA #3

Virus Core Requirements: 3 "A," 2 "B," and 1 "Q"

After returning from his journey with Mistral, it's time to let BlackRose know that Kite has the missing Virus Core. Log out of the "The World" and check email. Respond to BlackRose's email by informing her that the gate can now be hacked. Kite may have also received a request for a gathering from Gardenia. Although he promised to meet her whenever she sends for him, ignore the message for the time being. Check the Board for new posts and pay special attention to the "Let's Play Tag" thread, as there should be another gob challenge awaiting Kite's attention.

Sender: BlackRose
Subject: Hey

Anything on your side?

Sender: Gardenia
No Subject

Going to Θ: Beautiful, Someone's, Treasure Gem.

Thread: Let's Play Tag   **Author: Albert**
Post: Whatever

You guys are all wussies. What does eavesdropping and food have anything to do with this gob?

I'm Alber the Early Bird, one of the Four Gob Kings gob!!! I've been up since 5AM! Come to

Δ: Detestable, Golden, New Truth at 6AM gob!

Come along gob!

TAKE THIS GIFT

Withdraw any Heavy Blade weapons from Kite's inventory at the Elf's Haven. Hold onto them until Kite can give them to BlackRose.

Once back in Highland City Dun Loireag, track down Cleama and trade him for the Lavaman Spear. Return to the Chaos Gate and invite BlackRose and Gardenia to join Kite. Give the Lavaman Spear to Gardenia and hack the gate blocking the area BlackRose had learned of.

Θ: CURSED, DESPAIRED, PARADISE

RECOMMENDED PARTY: KITE, BLACKROSE, AND GARDENIA

AREA VITALS	
BATTLE LEVEL:	20
ELEMENT:	Darkness
GRUNTY FOOD:	La Pumpkin
	Bloody Egg
ENVIRONMENT:	Grassland
WEATHER:	Night

MONSTERS
FIELD:
Fire Witch: Fire
Wood Harpy: Wood
Lambada Knife
DUNGEON:
Fire Witch: Fire
Dark Witch: Darkness
Wood Harpy: Wood
Lambada Knife

ITEMS	
Dark Night	Fire Helm
Blaze Armor	Lavaman Spear
Fireman's Coat	Water God Axe
The Lovers	Nightblight
Virus Core A	Antidote
Fire Dance Hat	Restorative
Firedrake Mail	Cooked Bile

BlackRose
Well, this is different...

The area that was gated off from the general gaming public is actually an infected grassland sunk deep into the blackness of night. Although the monsters lurking here are somewhat weak and susceptible to the Tiger Claw skill, it's important for the party's well being that every monster be slain—BlackRose and Gardenia need the EXP!

It's been a while since Kite has adventured with BlackRose and he likely has several Heavy Blade weapons to give her. BlackRose is a much fiercer warrior with the Shanato or Byakuen.

As was the case with the snow-covered areas, those set at night have more than their fair share of Symbols. Kite and his allies will seldom be without at least three or four simultaneous increases in stats. While the Symbols no doubt help, use any remaining Burning Oil and Pure Water items to increase the party's Fire and Water ratings. The area's toughest foe, the Fire Witches, can be disposed of quickly but their magic is quite powerful.

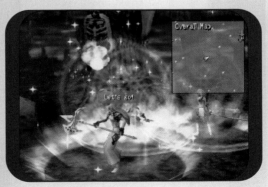

Let's go!

Dungeon, B1

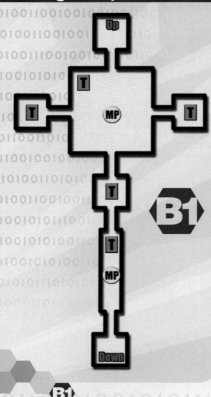

Dungeon, B2

Each floor in this dungeon is small and very straightforward, making this one of the quicker dungeons to navigate. The enemies found within these halls are similar to those outside, but the party will encounter the Dark Witch in addition to the Fire Witch. Equip the Spell Blades to unleash the Lightning Rage skill on the Dark Witch—sticking with the Tiger Claw will work equally well.

Smash each Egg in the small side rooms on this floor, because many of them contain **Cooked Bile**. This item not only increases the Darkness rating, but it's also valuable in trade with several of the other players. There is no need to use it in this area.

Dungeon, B3

The party encounters the final Magic Portal in the dungeon just beyond the staircase. Continue north through the next room to an area unlike any other. Without warning, Kite and BlackRose step blindly into a boundless white space, containing nothing but a canopy bed and a large assemblage of children's toys—stuffed animals to be exact.

Kite reads through Harald's Note and learns of a girl named Aura, who is charged with being a savior… but to whom? Further inspection of the room reveals **Epitaph 00**, although it doesn't aid in comprehending this overwhelming madness. Kite believes the "shining girl" referred to in Harald's Note is none other than the girl who gave him the bracelet. The party then returns to Root Town, not knowing any more now than before they left.

RAISING
A GRUNTY

ADDITIONAL
ELEMENTS

TRADE
LIST

BOOKS
OF RYU

BESTIARY

GARDENIA'S REQUEST

Kite's time online in "The World" is getting stranger with each passing area, yet Orca remains in his coma and Kite must continue to push ahead for a recovery. If Kite is to ever get to the bottom of Orca's illness, he must trust in those he meets online. The time has come to head off with Gardenia to the area of her choosing.

RAISING GRUNTIES

This is a great time to begin raising Grunties, as Kite is likely to have at least a handful of each food variety in his inventory. See the "Raising a Grunty" chapter for a detailed listing of each food's effects, as well as the final attributes required to raise a Noble Grunty, Poison Grunty, and Iron Grunty.

 Θ: BEAUTIFUL, SOMEONE'S, TREASURE GEM

RECOMMENDED PARTY: KITE, GARDENIA, AND MIA

AREA VITALS

BATTLE LEVEL:	18
ELEMENT:	Wood
GRUNTY FOOD:	Mandragora
	Golden Egg
	Immature Egg
ENVIRONMENT:	Grassland
WEATHER:	Sunny

MONSTERS

FIELD:
Phantom Wing
Menhir: Thunder
Noisy Wisp: Darkness

DUNGEON:
Menhir: Thunder
Dark Witch: Darkness
Noisy Wisp: Darkness
Phantom Wing

ITEMS

Virus Core B	Health Drink
Virus Core A	Holy Sap
Green Gale	Gale Breath
Fire Helm	Fireman's Coat
Earth Rod	Newt Necklace
Fire Dance Hat	The Fool
Restorative	The Devil

GOTT STATUE ITEMS

Graceful Book
Silver Scarab (x2)

The party arrives in a grassy hillside with a burning sunset in the distance. Gardenia wonders aloud whether or not the Hitorishizuka grows in this area. Kite teases her about her romantic sentiments, then leads them toward their first battle.

There are lots of Menhirs in this journey across the field, so equip the Bloody Blades and unleash the Twin Darkness skill to put them down with an Elemental Hit. Always go for the Menhir first so it can't resurrect its fellow monsters.

The toughest situation to arise in this field occurs when two Menhirs are encountered simultaneously. Since they can quickly resurrect one another, it's important to kill the second one quickly. The best way to handle them is to issue the "Operation Union Battle" strategy and gang up on one Menhir. Issue the "Skills!" command to the others, but make sure Kite has at least 45 SP. As soon as the first Menhir drops, rush the other one and use the Twin Darkness skill to destroy it before it can resurrect its fallen friend.

WHAT GOES UP...

Since the more powerful physical attack skills require 45 SP, Kite will likely need to rely on the Tiger Claw skill frequently. When attacking a Noisy Wisp with this skill, wait for it to descend closer to the ground before unleashing the attack. Since the Noisy Wisp has the ability to fly, it can occasionally get too high for the attack to be successful.

Although this area is Wood-based, most of the enemies here are aligned with Thunder and Darkness. Although it's best to keep Kite equipped with the Bloody Blades, switch to the Spell Blades when in need of a Lightning skill to attack the Noisy Wisps.

Kite can collect numerous Mandragoras in this field, in addition to **Gold** and **Silver Axes** from Grandpa at the Spring of Myst. There aren't many Treasures to open in this area, and the enemies rarely yield anything other than a Virus Core when Data Drained. Nevertheless, the additional EXP will help the group become stronger and the additional time spent with Gardenia and Mia will increase their affection toward Kite.

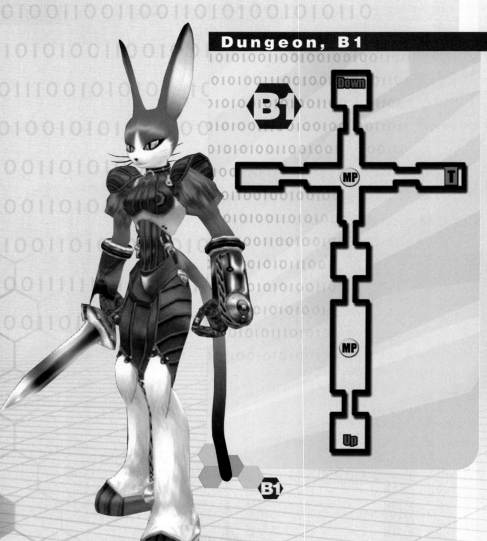

Dungeon, B1

The first floor of the dungeon is very small and contains just two Magic Portals. Smash all of the urns in the eastern room near the intersection to yield numerous Holy Saps. Although most of the weaponry collected in this area is Fire-based, the items and scrolls are almost all Wood-based. Collect as many Holy Saps as possible and trade them for powerful items later.

RAISING
A GRUNTY

ADDITIONAL
ELEMENTS

TRADE
LIST

BOOKS
OF RYU

BESTIARY

Dungeon, B2

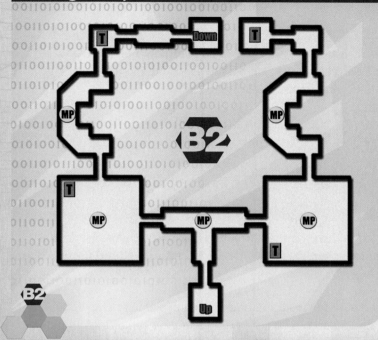

The second floor of the dungeon is much larger than the first floor, plus it contains multiple Magic Portals and Treasures. Fortunately, most of the Magic Portals in this dungeon contain Treasures and not enemies! Head east at the intersection and explore the path leading north to collect the Treasures and Grunty Food near the dead end.

Dungeon, B3

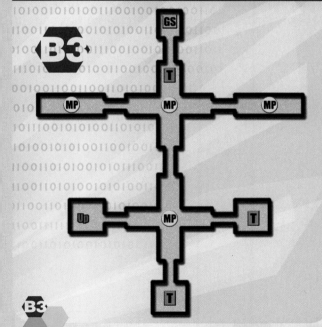

The action gets going quite fiercely on the third floor. The first Magic Portal encountered contains numerous Phantom Wings and Dark Wisps. Issue the "Skills!" command and use the Tiger Claw skill to dish out lots of damage to multiple monsters at once.

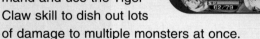

Smash the crates in the room to the south, then explore each of the lengthy halls to the north for more enemies and EXP. After clearing the dungeon of Magic Portals, head to the far northern end of the dungeon to gather the items from the Gott Statue. There, Kite can gain the **Graceful Book**, which provides a +1 permanent increase to the user's physical accuracy rating.

ORCA'S RUMOR

Kite is given an email notification after finishing his exploits with Gardenia. After this occurs, log out of "The World" and read the email from BlackRose. The "Missing" thread on the Board concerns her, so she's looking into it. While BlackRose is busy playing cybersleuth, log back into "The World" and check the Board.

> ✉ **Thread: To Orca**   **Author: Bob**
> **Post: It's Bob**
>
> I'm late, but I got that thing you wanted. I'll be at the area you said you'll take your friend.
>
> PS: Mailer seems to be hiccupping, so I wrote here. Hope it's not a problem.

Although Bob didn't come right out and say it, he was referring to the area that Orca had taken Kite before his fateful accident. Enter the game and warp to the Δ server. Once there, select the keywords Δ: **Bursting, Passed Over, Aqua Field**. Don't worry about bringing any friends; this is a short trip.

Kite meets Bob, a Long Arm, on the field where Orca had earlier taught Kite the basics. Kite explains to Bob that Orca had been Data Drained. Bob thinks that Orca met his tragic ending as a result of investigating the rumor that something weird was going on inside "The World." Bob had heard another player named Linda talking to Orca about it. Bob not only lets Kite know that Linda is at Δ: **Buried, Pagan, Fiery Sands**, but he hands over a book titled **Secret: Reason**. This book adds +2 to Kite's Magical Defense rating. Upon returning to Root Town, save at the Recorder and invite Mia and Elk to join the party. Head off together to the area where Bob last saw Linda.

△: BURIED, PAGAN, FIERY SANDS
RECOMMENDED PARTY: KITE, MIA, AND ELK

AREA VITALS
BATTLE LEVEL: 22
0111001000101010101110101101010
ELEMENT: Fire
0111001000101010111010110100010
GRUNTY FOOD: Oh No Melon
Bloody Egg
Golden Egg
0111001000101010111010110100010
ENVIRONMENT: Desert
0111001000101010111010110100010
WEATHER: Very Hot
0111001000101010111010110100010

MONSTERS
FIELD:
0111001001010101011110
Fire Witch: Fire
Gladiator: Thunder
Hell Box
DUNGEON:
0111001001010101011110
Lambada Knife
Fire Witch: Fire
Gladiator: Thunder
Fresh Valkyrie: Wood
Hell Box

ITEMS
Aqua Guard	Ice Hunter Cap
Snow Panther	Lavaman Spear
Virus Core A	Healing Potion
Raccoon Earcap	The Moon
Hands of Wood	Restorative
Fuse Blades	Antidote
Defense Sword	The Lovers
The Hanged Man	Meteor Swarm
Fire Tempest	Burning Oil

GOTT STATUE ITEMS
Smith's Gloves
Grunt Doll
Yellow Candy

The battles in the field are full of various enemies including the Hell Box, which has the ability to inflict Confusion to all of the party members. Although the Fire Witch and Gladiators can't be ignored for long, it's important to issue the "Operation Union Battle" strategy to the party and gang up on the Hell Box whenever one is present. Keep a close eye on everyone's status and hand out Restoratives to Confused party members when necessary.

The Fire Witch and Gladiator have far less HP than the Hell Box and can be disposed of quickly with the Tiger Claws or Twin Darkness skill attacks. Of the two, the Fire Witch is the bigger threat because it can fire off magical attacks from a moderate distance. Conversely, the Gladiator can only attack at close range—albeit with great force.

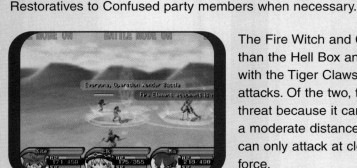

Dungeon, B1

The battles that waged on the field continue inside of the dungeon, but with far fewer Hell Boxes to worry about. Grab the **Golden Egg** at the forked room and explore the western halls before moving east.

RETURN VISIT RECOMMENDED

An event takes place on the second floor of the dungeon that ends with Kite returning to Root Town. Because all of the Magic Portals can't be cleared during Kite's first visit to this dungeon, there's no need to engage "out of the way" enemies on this first visit; just proceed through the dungeon to the steps leading down to B2.

Dungeon, B2

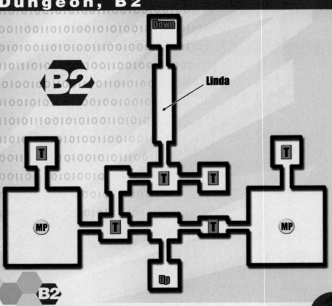

Use the Symbol near the entrance to this floor, then scout out each of the rooms to the far west and east to collect **Health Potions** and **Burning Oils**. Although you're likely to repeat the journey through these halls soon enough, don't pass up an opportunity to collect free Health Potions—they'll come in handy later on. Also, smash each egg and hold onto its booty for later.

Kite encounters Linda in the long corridor leading north to the stairs. Linda believes in the rumor and is convinced that there is something with a much larger purpose than gaming existing within "The World." However, she advises Kite to forget what he knows. If someone as powerful as Orca, one of the "Descendants of Fianna," can be defeated by the mysterious powers, surely Kite will fail as well. When Kite refuses to back down, Linda aids him by providing the address Δ: **Lonely, Silent, Great Seal**. Orca told Linda of a strange room in that area.

COME AGAIN?

Kite should immediately give the "Everyone Gather!" command and return to this area after meeting with Linda. Return straight to the dungeon and clear away all of the monsters from each Magic Portal and smash all of the eggs once again.

Dungeon, B3

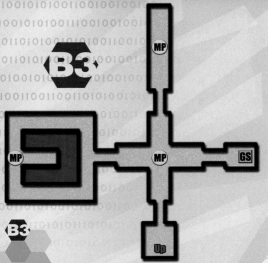

Put the Meteor Swarms to use against the Fresh Valkyries on the lowest floor of the dungeon. Make sure Kite has room in his inventory for the goodies to be gathered from the Gott Statue. Give any unusable items to Mia or Elk, then return to the surface with the newfound treasure.

RAISING
A GRUNTY

ADDITIONAL
ELEMENTS

TRADE
LIST

BOOKS
OF RYU

BESTIARY

PROTECTED AREA #4

Virus Core Requirements: 4 "B," 1 "C," and 1 "O"

Kite's next journey takes him to the area that Linda had told him about. Invite Elk and Gardenia to join the party and use the Chaos Gate to hack into the Protected Area.

△: LONELY, SILENT, GREAT SEAL

RECOMMENDED PARTY: KITE, ELK, AND GARDENIA

AREA VITALS	
BATTLE LEVEL:	22
ELEMENT:	Water
GRUNTY FOOD:	White Cherry
	Bear Cat Egg
	Golden Egg
ENVIRONMENT:	Snowfield
WEATHER:	Sunny

MONSTERS
FIELD:
Fresh Valkyrie: Wood
Living Dead: Darkness
Hell Box
DUNGEON:
Lamia Hunter: Earth
Living Dead: Darkness
Fresh Valkyrie: Wood
Baby Worm

ITEMS	
Komura	Healing Potion
The Fool	Pure Water
Ice Strike	Antidote
Virus Core A	The Devil
Virus Core B	Health Drink
Wyrm Scale	The Hanged Man
The Death	Restorative
Hands of Wood	Ice Storm
Resurrect	Amateur Blades
Ice Floe	Fishing Gloves

The party can use the Symbols in this snow-covered area to help them clear the field of its monsters. All three characters should be at or above Level 23 by the time they reach this area and, if Kite has been clearing every field and dungeon, he could even be at a higher level.

The only enemy making its first appearance here is the Living Dead creature. This Darkness-based creature is vulnerable to the Lightning Rage physical attack skill, so make sure Kite comes equipped with the Spell Blades.

SKIP THE DATA DRAIN

The enemies encountered in this area seldom yield anything other than Virus Core A when being Data Drained. Unless Kite is in need of Virus Cores or hasn't yet unlocked all eight Ryu Books, it's best to forego Data Draining to conserve the SP.

Dungeon, B1

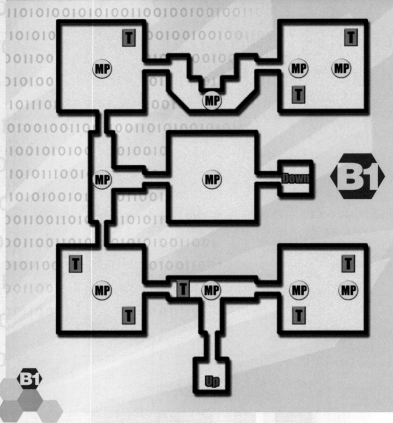

The dungeon in this area is crawling with an overly tall monstrosity called the Lamia Hunter. Although this species of enemy looks awkward, they are capable of an extremely quick slash and can attack from a distance thanks to their lengthy arms and weapon. It's best to have Gardenia and Elk focus on the Lamia Hunters while Kite deals with the enemies that don't have such an extensive reach.

The party can gain a lot of EXP by traveling to the large room in the northeastern corner of B1. They will encounter several Fresh Valkyries and Lamia Hunters here. Make sure everyone's health is topped off before entering the battle and position Kite in the thick of the fracas to inflict maximum damage with his Tiger Claws attack.

RAISING
A GRUNTY

ADDITIONAL
ELEMENTS

TRADE
LIST

BOOKS
OF RYU

BESTIARY

Dungeon, B2

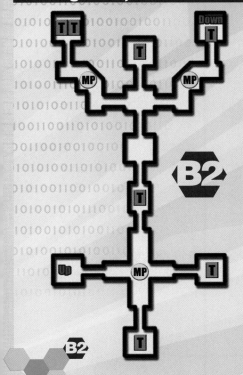

The second floor of the dungeon contains lots of Living Dead enemies. Their powerful mallets can immobilize anyone hit with them, so keep an eye on each party member's status and quickly administer an Antidote when necessary—an afflicted ally will glow yellow and will likely call out for help.

The party also encounters one of the largest enemies yet seen on this floor. Don't be fooled by its name—the Baby Worm is no runt! Since the Baby Worm isn't aligned with any of the elements, it's susceptible to any number of attacks. It will also take a lot to bring it down, as it has nearly 2000 HP! Issue the "Skills" command to Gardenia and Elk to get them involved. Have Kite mix in physical and magical skill attacks to lend a hand in bringing down the

beast. The one thing the party members must watch out for is the Baby Worm's spinning attack. It will quickly rotate in a circle in an attempt to bowl over anyone standing too close. Those hit by its tail will lose an average of 150 HP, so keep a safe distance when possible.

Dungeon, B3

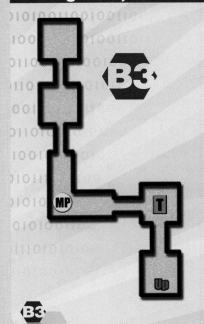

The party's exploration of the dungeon comes to an abrupt end just a few rooms north of the staircase on B3. Kite finds himself in another vacant white room completely void of monsters, textures, or sounds. The only object in the room is a rocking chair and, oddly enough, it has a large bite taken out of it. In fact, whatever had bitten through the chair had done so to a portion of the floor as well. Kite also discovers a note titled "**Epitaph ?**" but he can't read it. He then returns to Root Town utterly confused and without any additional leads.

A MEETING WITH MEG

 Sender: BlackRose
Subject: Found a Clue!

00110011001101010010101001100010011

I succeeded in contacting Alf's friend. I'm meeting up with Meg at Θ: Great, Distant, Fertile Land so why don't you come as well.

Let's pray there's something.

Log back into "The World" and warp to the Θ server. BlackRose will be waiting by the Chaos Gate. Invite her and Mia to join Kite in the trip to meet Meg.

Θ: GREAT, DISTANT, FERTILE LAND

RECOMMENDED PARTY: KITE, BLACKROSE, AND MIA

AREA VITALS

BATTLE LEVEL: 23
ELEMENT: Darkness
GRUNTY FOOD: La Pumpkin
Bloody Egg
Golden Egg
ENVIRONMENT: Wasteland
WEATHER: Stormy

MONSTERS

FIELD:
Hell Box
Lamia Hunter: Earth
Grand Mage: Fire

DUNGEON:
Grand Mage: Fire
Hell Box
Lamia Hunter: Earth
Armor Shogun
Baby Worm

ITEMS

The Hanged Man	The Lovers
The Moon	Strormer Spear
Firedrake Mail	Singing Blade
Blaze Armor	Mage's Soul
Air Bracer	Antidote
Hands of Wood	Resurrect
Scarab Earring	Cooked Bile
Virus Core A	Healing Potion
Dark Night	Virus Core C
Nightblight	

GOTT STATUE ITEMS

Oak Anklet
Rainbow Card (x2)

The enemy types in this area are the toughest yet. Although Kite is already very familiar with the dangers posed by the Hell Box and the Lamia Hunter, the Grand Mage is deceivingly powerful. Not only is this master of the arcane quite fast (it takes a Speed Charm to chase him down), but his magic attacks are particularly deadly. The Grand Mage's one weakness is his relatively low HP. Chase after the Grand Mage and use the Staccato or Tiger Claws physical attack skill to cut him to shreds.

The potent magic of the Grand Mage combined with the Confusion caused by the Hell Box and the long blade of the Lamia Hunter makes for plenty of battles that must rely on the "First Aid!" command. Make sure the other party members have plenty of Resurrects and don't hesitate to take over their actions if Kite falls in battle.

The keywords for this area combined to make an environment highly conducive to the presence of La Pumpkins, Symbols, and a Spring of Myst that will increase the level of a weapon or armor. Take advantage of these benefits before entering the dungeon.

Dungeon, B1

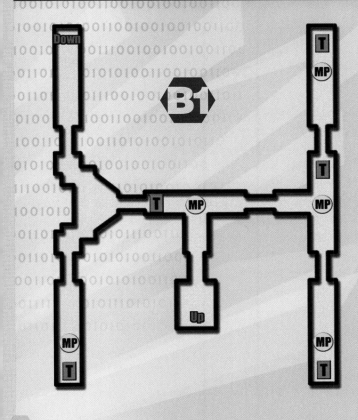

The Magic Portals in the rooms in the eastern part of the floor contain a new type of enemy called the Armor Shogun. These enormous warriors carry enormous samurai swords and they have the skills to use them. What's worse is that they are often accompanied by a Grand Mage, who will increase the Fire rating. Avoid the tendency to engage the giant Armor Shoguns until after the Grand Mage has been slain. With any luck, the Staccato attack will damage multiple enemies at once.

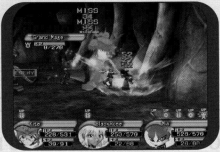

Dungeon, B2

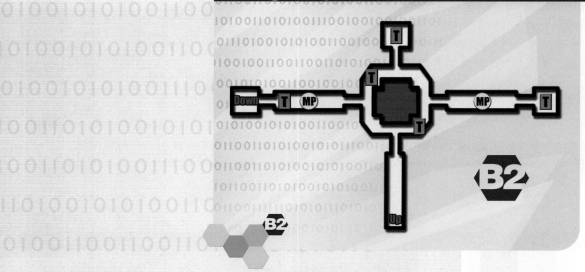

Dungeon, B3

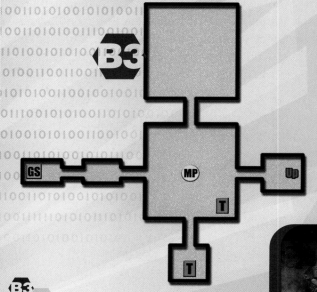

Clear the monsters from the final Magic Portal, then head to the room to the west to collect the items from the Gott Statue. After opening the Treasure, head north to find Meg. A man who BlackRose and Kite presume to be Alf warps out of the dungeon just as the party arrives. BlackRose has been trying to track him down for some time via the Board and asks Meg to tell her where Alf went. Meg tells the pair that the keywords can be found on the Board and the area is very dangerous. Armed with this newfound information, Kite and BlackRose return to Root Town.

RAISING
A GRUNTY

ADDITIONAL
ELEMENTS

TRADE
LIST

BOOKS
OF RYU

BESTIARY

PROTECTED AREA #5

Virus Core Requirements: 1 "A," 4 "B," 1 "C," and 1 "P"

Log out of the game and check the Board to see what Meg has posted. There's a new message in the "Missing" thread that has been deleted. Did someone delete Meg's post? Exit back to the desktop. Once there, Kite receives an email notification. BlackRose noticed the deleted post too and she's fighting mad about it. There's not a whole lot to do right now, so log back into "The World."

Take advantage of this "down time" by inviting different pairs of players to join in adventures to random areas. Use the Random Keyword option at the Chaos Gate to warp to new areas with different monsters and items. Not only is this a great way to gain additional EXP and weaponry before fighting the game's final boss, but it's also a great way to increase the other characters' affection rating for Kite. Data Drain every type of enemy encountered in this random search to gain items that may have otherwise gone uncollected.

Kite then receives another email notification. Log out of "The World" and check the email program on the desktop. Kite obtains another scrambled plea for help from Aura, but more importantly, a letter from Helba, who copied and pasted Meg's original post into the email. Whoever Helba is, she sure wants Kite to succeed. Or is she setting a trap?

CONGRATULATORY EMAILS

Kite receives a congratulatory email upon defeating the game from any of the players who reach the maximum affection rating of 250. Kite can quickly maximize each player's feelings toward him by giving them valuable items and by spending more time with them in battle. Additionally, Kite can raise their affection by giving them less valuable potions and scrolls one at a time.

Sender: Helba
Subject: Dear Kite

0011001100110101001010100110010011

This is the deleted post:

Meg

Θ: Chosen, Hopeless, Nothingness

He said he saw a girl and guy with a red wand playing tag. I received an e-mail from Alf's family, which said he slipped into a coma while playing the game.

The data volume is increasing in Θ: Chosen, Hopeless, Nothingness.

Not surprisingly, BlackRose is at Highland City Dun Loireag when Kite arrives. And despite Kite's warning that "IT" might be there, BlackRose demands to accompany him to the restricted area. Invite Gardenia to accompany the duo and begin to prepare for the final area.

Store all unnecessary items at the Elf's Haven, then head to the Item Shop and purchase several of each of the Blood potions, as well as a healthy supply of Mage's Souls, Resurrects, and Health Drinks. Sell off some of the weaker armor and weaponry if necessary, but keep at least a dozen Mage's Soul and Resurrects, and no less than 20 Health Drinks. Also, give BlackRose and Gardenia a few Resurrects.

Θ: CHOSEN, HOPELESS, NOTHINGNESS

RECOMMENDED PARTY: KITE, BLACKROSE, AND GARDENIA

AREA VITALS	
BATTLE LEVEL:	28
ELEMENT:	Earth
GRUNTY FOOD:	Root Vegetable
	Immature Egg
	Golden Egg
ENVIRONMENT:	Grassland
WEATHER:	Night

MONSTERS
FIELD:
Cursed Blades
Mantis: Water
Metal Goblin: Earth
DUNGEON:
Cursed Blades
Mu Guardian: Earth
Mantis: Water
Red Scissors: Water
Goil Menhir: Thunder
Ogre: Fire

ITEMS	
Sleipner	Bom-Ba-Ye
Virus Core A	Restorative
Anshou	Well Water
Blaze Armor	Stone Storm
Jinsaran	The Death
Fireman's Coat	Virus Core B
Raining Rocks	Axe Bomber
Mage's Soul	The Lovers
Raging Earth	Resurrect
The Devil	Healing Potion
Electric Guard	Smith's Gloves
The Hanged Man	Fire Bracer
Antidote	Iron Anklet

Rated at Level 28, this is by far the toughest area yet. Because of this, specific tactics should be employed for nearly every enemy encounter. Not only will this help ensure the group's success, but it will also help them gain EXP while at the same time minimizing the number of recovery items they consume. It's wise to Data Drain every enemy at least twice to get better weapons for the entire party. Similarly, use Repth and La Repth instead of Health Drinks whenever possible. Finally, avoid using a Mage's Soul or Health Potion while in the field, as they are more important later in the dungeon.

The toughest enemy in this field is the Water-based Mantis. However, the Masterblades' Twin Dragons physical attack skill will make short work of it. Give BlackRose and Gardenia the "Skills!" command and allow them to eliminate the Cursed Blades and Metal Goblin.

Since these battles earn the group so much EXP, and the upcoming dungeon crawl is loaded with vicious beasts, you may want to clear this field twice. Use a Fairy's Orb to spot all of the Magic Portals, defeat every enemy on the map, then gate out back to Root Town. Once there, save at the Recorder and reenter the area to do it all again—this extra effort will pay off later! Gate out after clearing the field a second time to save once more, then use the Grunty Flute to get a quick ride to the dungeon's entrance when the group is ready to head underground.

LEVEL 30

Characters at Level 28 can successfully destroy the boss that resides at the end of this level, but it's not easy. However, characters at Level 30 or higher will have a much easier time. The extra HP and SP will not go to waste!

Dungeon, B1

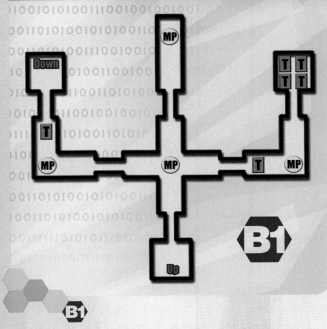

EQUIPMENT CHOICE

Equip the Masterblades for Kite's weapon and the Scarab Earring for his head armor. The Masterblades contains two powerful physical attack skills, while the Scarab Earring grants its wearer the ability to bring back a fallen ally from the grave. The Rip Maen skill consumes a lot of SP, but it will save its wearer from using a Resurrect.

The group fights even more Mantis and Cursed Blades enemies inside the dungeon, but they will soon be face-to-face with the Mu Guardian as well. This Earth-based robotic beast should be handled with Wood-based skills or powerful physical attack skills such as the Staccato.

Dungeon, B2

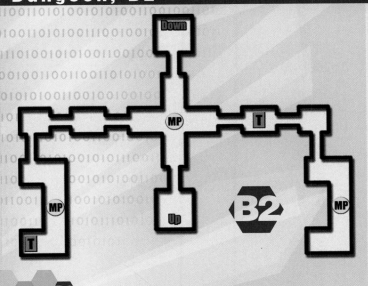

The party encounters more Mu Guardians on the second floor, so have Kite use any Wood-based magic skills at his disposal, such as the Juk Kruz from equipping the Holy Tree Mail. Soon, the Mu Guardians are accompanied by Goil Menhirs. As noted previously, destroying Menhirs is always the number one priority since they can revive fallen creatures. Switch to the Anshou weapon and use its Twin Darkness skill against the Goil Menhir to destroy it.

Dungeon, B3

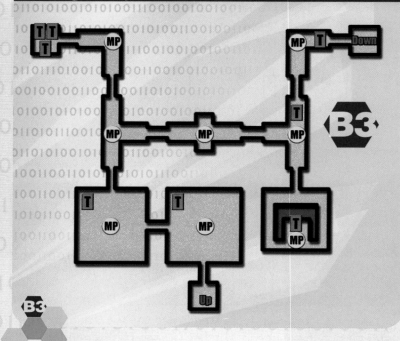

Switch back to Kite's Masterblades on B3 to prepare for a new enemy called the Red Scissors. Use the Twin Dragons skill to slash through the Red Scissors for an Elemental Hit. Continue to switch back and forth between the Anshou and the Masterblades based on whether Kite is going up against a Mantis and Red Scissors or a Goil Menhir.

Dungeon, B4

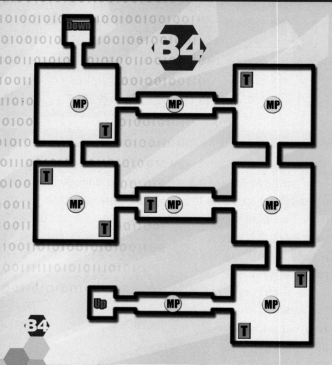

The dungeon's fourth floor is ruled by the Ogre, a Fire-based enemy with over 2200 HP! Since Kite likely doesn't have any Water-based skills, sit back and allow the other party members to engage the Ogre. Of course, use Kite's remaining Ice Strike scrolls in hopes of an Elemental Hit to help whittle down the beast's reserves. Kite may acquire the Masterblades by Data Draining the Ogre, so use the bracelet to hopefully acquire that powerful weapon.

RAISING
A GRUNTY

ADDITIONAL
ELEMENTS

TRADE
LIST

BOOKS
OF RYU

BESTIARY

Dungeon, B5

The lowest floor of the dungeon consists of a narrow corridor leading directly to the final boss's chamber. Stop outside the doorway with the purple gases escaping from the floor, and prepare for the difficult battle that lurks beyond the wall.

Give each party member a dose of Warrior Blood, Knight Blood, Hunter Blood, Hermit Blood, and Beast Blood, as well as Pure Water, Well Water, Burning Oil, Holy Tree Sap, and Cooked Bile. Buffing each character's stats and elemental defenses is an integral part of the strategy needed to defeat Skeith. Wait for everyone's SP to be replenished and cast any recovery spells to top off everyone's HP before walking through the doorway.

Kite arrives on the scene just in time to witness Aura, the girl who has been sending him the scrambled emails, be Data Drained by Skeith. Like Orca, Aura has been eliminated from the game environment.

FINAL BOSS BATTLE: SKEITH

level	99	**pp**	9000
hp	30000/3000	**sp**	999
element	N/A		
skills	Execution		
	Darkness		
	Judgement		
	Darkness (Epitaph)		
reward	Virus Core F		

Skeith is the most deadly creature the party has encountered in the game thus far. It's clear from the start of the battle that this beast requires a much different strategy than previous boss fights. For starters, Kite cannot rely on the others to keep him alive; instead he must act as the healer in this fight. Give the "Skills!" command as soon as the battle begins and allow BlackRose and Gardenia to rush in and use their physical attack skills. Kite must stay on the move during the battle to stay far enough away from Skeith to avoid his Execution attack and other close-range skills.

FINAL BOSS BATTLE: SKEITH

Keep a vigilant eye on the status of each ally and give them recovery items when needed—La Repth will most likely be ineffective, as Kite will be too far away to use it. As a general rule, give a Health Drink to any player who falls below 400 HP and a Healing Potion whenever they get below 200 HP. If the supply of Resurrects gets low, cast the Rip Maen skill.

Kite also needs to keep up a steady attack using scrolls. Dish out attacks with the Stone Storm, Raging Earth, and Green Gale scrolls so that Skeith is continuously taking damage. Kite can use these scrolls from a great distance and still be an active part of the battle.

Of course, Skeith isn't going to sit back and let the threesome pound away on him. Skeith's most dangerous attack is his Judgement skill. This attack freezes all three party members in separate blocks of ice, regardless of their position, and delivers between 150 and 400 HP of damage. Since Skeith will employ this attack multiple times, it's very important to administer a Pure Water to anyone who needs to be brought back to life. There's no buff more valuable during this battle than the Pure Water, as it halves the damage suffered by the Ice Magic skill.

Skeith has one other major trick up his sleeve: the use of his own Data Drain powers. Although he won't destroy anyone as he did with Orca and Aura, he will raise BlackRose up on his cross and cause each of her attributes to lower. Kite must act quickly and give her a Restorative and Antidote to counter the lowering of her various abilities to make her fit for battle.

If Kite succeeds in keeping everyone alive and maintains a steady barrage of scroll attacks against Skeith, he will eventually get the chance to Data Drain the beast. Once Skeith has been Data Drained, his post-Data Drain state will be reduced to just 3000 HP and he won't use the deadly attacks he used earlier. What makes finishing off the battle difficult is Skeith's speed. Nevertheless, if the group continues their assault as noted here, the creature will soon fall.

SPOILER FREE ENDING!

Although we won't reveal what happens after Skeith is defeated, it should be noted that Kite's quest is far from over. Follow the on-screen instructions to make a "flagged data file" that can be imported into the next volume in the .hack series, then return to the desktop to check for emails from "Roy@Bandai." Flip ahead to the "Side Quests" chapter for help with the bonus adventures that await.

RAISING
A GRUNTY

ADDITIONAL
ELEMENTS

TRADE
LIST

BOOKS
OF RYU

BESTIARY

SIDE QUESTS

GOBLIN TAG—ROUND ONE: STEHONEY

△: DETESTABLE, GOLDEN, SUNNY DEMON

AREA VITALS	
BATTLE LEVEL:	1
ELEMENT:	Wood
GRUNTY FOOD:	Mandragora
ENVIRONMENT:	Grassland
WEATHER:	Partly Cloudy

MONSTERS
Stehoney: Earth

ITEMS
Goblin Cap

Stehoney (190 HP) is waiting on the hilltop in the field. Before Kite can even introduce himself, Stehoney challenges Kite to a game of tag. To win, Kite must chase after Stehoney and slash at him until his HP gets reduced to zero.

Stehoney may just be an apprentice to the four Gob Kings, but he's still quite fast. For that reason, use a Speed Charm. The increased speed will enable Kite to get close enough to slash at the goblin. Although items and skills can be used in the game of tag, it's good practice for later to rely solely on basic weapons attacks. As you'll see, chasing down a goblin at high speeds is a great way to master the camera controls!

Although Stehoney is fast, that is the extent of his abilities. Not only will he not heal himself, but he won't raise a sword in defense either. Continue chasing after Stehoney until he drops. He'll then award Kite with his prize, the **Goblin Cap**. Although the Goblin Cap isn't as beneficial as Kite's original head armor, store it at the Elf's Haven for later use.

GOBLIN TAG—ROUND TWO: JONUE THE GOBBLER

△: DETESTABLE, GOLDEN, MESSENGER

AREA VITALS	
BATTLE LEVEL:	6
ELEMENT:	Fire
GRUNTY FOOD:	Oh No Melon
ENVIRONMENT:	Desert
WEATHER:	Sunny

MONSTERS
Jonue: Earth

ITEMS
Goblin Mail

Jonue
Try me. "Jonue the Gobbler," one
of the Four Gob Kings!!

FREE FRESH FRUIT

This is a great place to stock up on Oh No Melons for Grunties. Don't gate out right after defeating Jonue—run around and gather up some melons first!

Jonue (330 HP) has considerably more HP than Stehoney, but Kite is much stronger now. To make quick work of Jonue, cast a Speed Charm as soon as the game begins. This should enable Kite to easily keep up with the goblin and chop him down to size one swipe at a time. For added efficiency, consider using a Warrior's Blood to increase Kite's attack rating. Or, for even more deadly results, use the Tiger Claw attack. Two strikes with the Tiger Claw will reduce Jonue to almost nothing. Kite receives the **Goblin Mail** for winning this round of tag. Return to the Elf's Haven and store it there for later.

GOBLIN TAG—ROUND THREE: EAVESDROPPING ZYAN

△: DETESTABLE, GOLDEN, SCENT

AREA VITALS	
BATTLE LEVEL:	10
ELEMENT:	Water
GRUNTY FOOD:	White Cherry
ENVIRONMENT:	Snowfield
WEATHER:	Snowing

MONSTERS
Zyan: Earth

ITEMS
Goblin Gloves

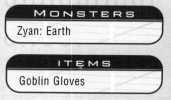

Zyan
Playing tag with me is not a
game anymore.

By the time Zyan's challenge comes around, Kite should be at a much higher level; therefore, there's not much to worry about. Utilize a Speed Charm to increase Kite's speed and unleash physical attack skills against Zyan (470 HP) when he draws near.

GOBLIN TAG-ROUND FOUR: ALBERT THE EARLY BIRD

△: DETESTABLE, GOLDEN, NEW TRUTH

AREA VITALS	
BATTLE LEVEL:	14
ELEMENT:	Earth
GRUNTY FOOD:	Root Vegetable
ENVIRONMENT:	Grassland
WEATHER:	Clear

MONSTERS
Albert: Earth

ITEMS
Goblin Boots

The first three rounds of Goblin Tag were merely a warm up for the final two rounds, which are both much more difficult. Switch to the Ronin Blades to have access to the Gale of Swords skill and have a Speed Charm handy. Albert (750 HP) has significantly more HP than the previous goblin, and he's also much faster and agile.

After using the Speed Charm, take a brief run after Albert, then stop and line the camera up with him as he leaves the battle area and comes to a stop in the distance. Use a Knight Blood or Holy Sap to increase Kite's effectiveness against the goblin. Dash after him and press the △ button to access the Personal Menu as soon as Kite gets close enough to attack. Use the Gale of Swords physical attack skill to chop him down. Depending on Kite's experience level, this attack may be enough to defeat Albert. If not, continue chasing after him and use the Tiger Claw skill to finish him off.

CHASING ANGLES

Keep the camera zoomed out when chasing after Albert. This provides the best vantage point to see his movements and realize when Kite is within striking range.

GOBLIN TAG-ROUND FIVE: MARTINA

△: DETESTABLE, GOLDEN, GATE

AREA VITALS	
BATTLE LEVEL:	23
ELEMENT:	Wood
GRUNTY FOOD:	Mushroom
ENVIRONMENT:	Leaf Mold
WEATHER:	Sunny

MONSTERS
Martina: Wood

ITEMS
Imp's Pin

After completing the game, return to the Board to check for new sets of keywords. As long as Kite won the first four rounds of Goblin Tag, there will be a final challenge.

> **Thread: Let's Play Tag**
> **Post: Oh?**   **Author: Martina**
>
> Oh, nooooo. They're all defeated gob? And I'm the only one left gob? Eeek! Scary gob. I'll be at
> Δ: Detestable, Golden, Gate gob.
> Come alone gob!

The fifth and final round of Goblin Tag takes place against Martina (890 HP), the fastest and most powerful goblin of all. As if keeping up with this gob wasn't difficult enough, Martina uses the powers of the Rig Seam skill to replenish her HP over time—17 HP every several seconds to be exact!

Kite's best chance to defeat Martina is to use a Speed Charm, then use physical attack skills such as Swirling Dark or Staccato to freeze her and get numerous attacks in at once. Since Martina has a relatively high physical evasion rating, Kite may miss many of his attacks, hence the need for an elaborate skill attack. Press the ⬠ button the moment the attack ends to immediately freeze Martina and unleash another attack. Continue doing this until Kite runs out of SP (use a Mage's Soul to replenish it) or until Martina slips away.

Eventually, Martina's HP replenishment skill will expire. As long as Kite stays on the goblin's heels, she won't be able to cast another Rig Seam. However, if Martina eludes Kite and manages to get outside the battle radius, she will cast the recovery spell again. For this reason, it's important to slowly whittle away Martina's HP and prevent her from getting out of Kite's reach once the spell runs out. It's not easy but with a bit of patience and some fancy footwork, it can be done!

Unlike the previous rounds of Goblin Tag, winning against Martina earns Kite the **Imp's Pin**, which is one of the Key Items in the game. With this item, Kite can equip the entire Goblin Series of armor (Goblin Cap, Goblin Mail, Goblin Gloves, and Goblin Boots) and access the Summon Goblin skill! Kite can call upon a Goblin to attack any nearby enemies.

THE ZEIT STATUE

> **Thread: Zeit Statue**
> **Post: Aim for Hero of Zeit!**   **Author: Admin of Time**
>
> Does everyone know about the Zeit Statue?
>
> The Zeit Statue at the bottom of the dungeon is searching for an adventurer to give a title of honor as the "Hero of Zeit."
>
> One way to get the title is to get to the Zeit Statue as fast as you can!
>
> Those who want the praise of the Zeit Statue select Chronicling as your part A at the Chaos Gate.
>
> *First look for an area with a dungeon close to the entrance and that doesn't have that many floors. The Hero of Zeit must also be versed in looking for an advantageous area.

This challenge, which can be completed at any time during the game, is open to all players. However, it is best left until Kite reaches Level 20 or higher. The goal of this challenge is to assemble a set of keywords that yields an area with a small dungeon and few enemies that can be raced through as fast as possible. Kite must sprint through the dungeon to the Zeit Statue as fast as possible to be ranked in the top five and receive the appropriate items.

HERO OF ZEIT RANKINGS

PLACE	TITLE	TIME	PLAYER	ITEM
First Place	Master Supreme	2:12	Balmung	Time Blades
Second Place	Hyper Falcon	2:26	Orca	Time Sandals
Third Place	Sonic Hawk	2:54	Sieg	Time Bracers
Fourth Place	Mach Wolf	3:38	Highlander	Time Sash
Fifth Place	Furious Tiger	4:45	NOG	Time Headband

There are a number of different keywords to use to complete this objective, but some are easier than others. For example, try **Δ: Chronicling, Pagan, Sunny Demon**. This dungeon is four floors deep, but the entrance to the dungeon is near the starting point. This means that Kite must enter only two battles to reach the Zeit Statue.

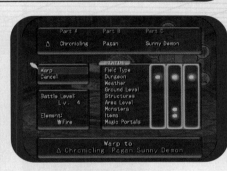

THE AERIAL FLEET

After completing the game, Kite receives a pair of emails from Roy@Bandai. The first email is about creating a flagged game save file. The second, however, contains the keywords to a secret area. Read the email shown below to gain access to this secret world.

Sender: Roy@Bandai
Subject: Giant of Heavens
OO11OO11OO11O1O1OO

Have you seen the Mystical Giant in the heavens of Δ areas?!

According to rumors, the aerial fleet transporting the Giant thousands of years ago was in an accident and now wanders with the giant forever.

Δ: Hideous, Someone's, Someone's Giant

Use this keyword to solve the mystery of the cursed fleet wandering in the heavens!

PS: I forgot to tell you, but I added a Virus Core T in your items.

FLEET-FOOTED TIPS

For starters, take a dry run through the dungeon to ensure you know where to go and what to expect. Then exit back out to Root Town and warp back to the area. Immediately use a Speed Charm, then head northwest to enter the dungeon—don't fight while in the field!

B1: Head south to the circular room with four doors. Head west and descend to B2.

B2: Continue south through the circular room to the stairs leading down to B3.

B3: Once at the "T," quickly eliminate the monsters, head west, and descend to B4.

B4: Kill the monsters and head west at the first turn.

Run up to the Zeit Statue and press the ⊗ button to stop the clock. Kite receives a reward based on the criteria in the previous table. Lay claim to the top spot to earn the full set of Time-themed armor and weaponry, some of which has maximum accuracy and evasion ratings!

△: HIDEOUS, SOMEONE'S, GIANT

RECOMMENDED PARTY: KITE, BLACKROSE, AND PIROS

Virus Core Requirements: 1 "T"

AREA VITALS

BATTLE LEVEL:	30
ELEMENT:	Water
ENVIRONMENT:	Leaf Mold
WEATHER:	Sunny

MONSTERS

Tetra Armor: Thunder
Mu Guardian: Earth
Mystery Rock: Earth
Red Scissors: Water

ITEMS

Scarlet Autumn	Master's Axe
Ice Floe	Restorative
Devil's Axe	Pure Water
The Moon	Health Drink

After hacking the gate to the Aerial Fleet, the party members find themselves on the deck of one of the ships high in the air. Enter the doorway at the end of the walkway and work through the two floors of the ship to find the Parasite Dragon.

Aerial, B1

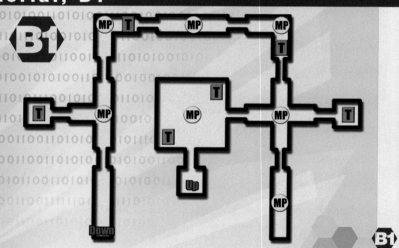

Aerial, B2

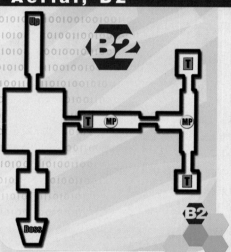

EXTRA BOSS: PARASITE DRAGON

level	30	**pp**	8888
hp	9999	**sp**	305
element	N/A		
skills	Breath High-Low		
reward	Hyakkidouran		

Although the battle against Skeith was definitely a challenge, the Parasite Dragon is arguably even tougher. The key to defeating this beast is to stand far away from it and allow BlackRose and Piros to charge in for melee combat. Since the Parasite Dragon has a Magic Tolerance, have Kite issue the "Attack!" command to prevent them from using any magical skills or items. Also, give Piros the Master's Axe or Devil's Axe before the battle. Don't forget to give BlackRose the Flame Sword either.

RAISING
A GRUNTY

ADDITIONAL
ELEMENTS

TRADE
LIST

BOOKS
OF RYU

BESTIARY

EXTRA BOSS: PARASITE DRAGON

The Parasite Dragon attacks swiftly and with great power, thereby mandating that one of the three remain out of reach to act as the designated healer. Kite must continue to use his Rip Maen skill and Resurrect potions to revive fallen allies. Also, have at least two dozen Health Drinks on hand and administer them whenever a character falls below 600 HP. Also, the Parasite Dragon has the ability to cause Confusion. When this occurs to the party, give them a Restorative.

Since Kite will be using the Rip Maen skill so often, BlackRose and Piros will likely die numerous times during this battle. Therefore, there's no reason to waste a Mage's Soul on either of the two attackers. It will be a long battle, but Kite must allow them to attack traditionally. Over time, the Parasite Dragon will have its HP whittled down to roughly 1000 HP, at which time it can be Data Drained. It's recommended that all party members be at least Level 31 before engaging the Parasite Dragon in battle.

OVA KEYWORDS

The anime disc included with *.hack//INFECTION* contains clues to special combinations of keywords. There are three sets of keywords to watch for, one of which is detailed below.

θ: DOG-DANCING, PASSIONATE, TRI PANSY

AREA VITALS	
BATTLE LEVEL:	19
ELEMENT:	Earth
ENVIRONMENT:	Grassland
WEATHER:	Sunny

MONSTERS
Menhir: Thunder
Dark Witch: Darkness
Noisy Wisp: Darkness
Phantom Wing

GOTT STATUE ITEMS
Ceramic Helm
Yellow Candy (x2)

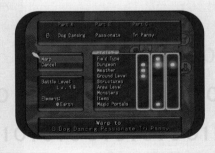

This is a great area to visit when Kite is around Level 20 and in need of a variety of items (such as Restoratives, Health Drinks, and Well Water). The main benefit this area offers is its wealth of Treasures and breakable objects, such as crates and barrels. Also, the **Ceramic Helm** is a rare item and, although a Twin Blade can't wear it, Kite can give it to BlackRose. This enables her to cast Rig Seam and Rig Geam before going into heavy battles.

RAISING A GRUNTY

Grunties are highly revered in "The World" and although they resemble a large pig, they can speak and trade just as well as any of the player characters. Once Kite reaches the Θ server and visits the Grunty Ranch, he'll have the opportunity to raise a Grunty from its childhood, through adolescence, and into adulthood. Raising a Grunty may seem simplistic at first—Kite only needs to feed it to help it grow—but a Grunty's stomach is very sensitive and the wrong food at the wrong time could stunt its growth.

READ THE BOARD

Everything you need to know about raising a Grunty is right in this section, but there is lots of information posted on the Board as well.

There are 16 varieties of Grunty Food to collect from the fields and dungeons in "The World" and each food type has a certain impact on the following characteristics of a Grunty: size, body odor, rebelliousness, brutality, intelligence, and purity. The Grunty's size is the most critical attribute, because it dictates when the Grunty matures. However, each category plays a role in determining the type of Grunty it will grow up to be.

Kite's interaction with his Grunty is pretty limited at first, for the Grunty will merely ask for food. While the Grunty is a "Little Grunty," its requests are very general and Kite should simply feed it whatever food types he has the most of. The food's effect is displayed in the data chart: the numbers in green show a positive effect, whereas the orange numbers reflect a decrease in the Grunty's rating for that attribute. Some food types will not affect every attribute. Continue feeding the Little Grunty until its size rating reaches 5. This is when it experiences its first growth spurt.

Once the Little Grunty begins to show signs of growth, its food requests become more specific. Talk to the Grunty to see what it would like to eat. At this stage, the Grunty will speak in abstract terms and will merely hint at what it would like to eat. Each request is followed by a vague description of where the food is located, such as "by a big cocoon." Although Kite can continue to feed the Grunty random food during this stage, it's much harder to raise an Iron Grunty or Poison Grunty if these requests aren't met. Use the table on the following page to decipher the Grunty's hints.

When the Grunty reaches a size rating of 10, it reaches adolescence and becomes Grunty the Kid. At this point, the Grunty starts to make specific requests for food. Although Kite can successfully raise a Noble Grunty by feeding the beast any food type, it's best to pay strict attention to the Grunty's requests and feed it the food it requires, even if it means collecting more food and returning with it at a later time. Grunty the Kid will undergo another growth spurt once it reaches a size rating of 20. Its final growth spurt occurs when it matures and becomes an Adult Grunty at size 30.

GRUNTY FOOD

	Food Type	Grunty Clue	Size	Body Odor	Rebel	Brutality	Intelligence	Purity	Controlling Keyword
	Cordyceps	Near a large statue of Buddha	+1	+2	+2	N/A	+2	+4	Part B: Someone's
	Grunt Mints	Near a very hot square face	+1	N/A	+4	-4	-2	-1	Part C: Great Seal
	La Pumpkin	Near a huge cocoon	+1	-3	-2	+3	+5	N/A	Part C: Paradise
	Mandragora	Near pointed towers	+1	+5	N/A	+4	-4	-4	Part C: Aqua Field
	Mushroom	In the shadow of mushroom boulders	+1	-4	-3	N/A	-3	-3	Part C: Hypha
	Oh No Melon	Near barnacles	+1	+3	+1	-1	+1	N/A	Part B: Destroyer's
	Piney Apple	Deep in the green forest	+1	N/A	-4	+5	+4	-2	Part B: Solitary
	Root Vegetable	By a wall at end of the labyrinth	+1	-2	-1	+2	N/A	+3	Part C: Fort Walls
	Snaky Cactus	Near ribs that were once an ocean	+1	+1	+5	-2	-1	+2	Part C: Fiery Sands
	Twilight Onion	Near a very strange old weapon	+1	+4	+3	-3	N/A	+1	Part B: Gluttonous
	White Cherry	Near a very cold pillar	+1	-1	N/A	+1	+3	+5	Part C: White Devil
	Bear Cat Egg	Deep in a very fancy gallery	+2	-1	-3	+1	+2	+3	N/A
	Bloody Egg	In stomach of a very scary monster	+2	+1	+3	N/A	-3	-1	N/A
	Golden Egg	A few grow inside an important story	+2	N/A	N/A	N/A	N/A	N/A	N/A
	Immature Egg	Deep in a very dark labyrinth	+2	-3	-1	+3	+2	+1	N/A
	Invisible Egg	Inside a very deep cave	+2	+3	+1	N/A	-1	-3	N/A

Once the Grunty reaches full size and matures into one of the three adult types (there are more types of Grunties in future volumes of *.hack*), Kite can trade with it for rare and valuable items. The tables on the following page show the requirements for each of the three Adult Grunties.

Noble Grunty

The Noble Grunty provides Kite with the **Grunty Flute**. This key item enables Kite to whistle for his pet when in the field on Θ server areas. The Noble Grunty will then swiftly carry Kite across the field free from the dangers of the monsters lurking in the Magic Portals.

ATTRIBUTE REQUIRED	RATING
Size	30
Body Odor	N/A
Rebel	N/A
Brutality	N/A
Intelligence	N/A
Purity	N/A

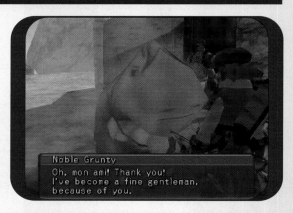

Noble Grunty
Oh, mon ami! Thank you!
I've become a fine gentleman,
because of you.

Poison Grunty

The Poison Grunty may not have any instruments to give Kite, but this creature does have some great weapons to trade for. Get the **Claymore** and **Charged Axe** from this kind of grunty—BlackRose and Piros will be ever so thankful!

ATTRIBUTE REQUIRED	RATING
Size	30
Body Odor	0 to 20
Rebel	-5 to 15
Brutality	10 to 30
Intelligence	5 to 25
Purity	-5 to 15

Poison Grunty
Ohh, master! Thank you ribbit!
Thanks to you I'm now an adult
ribbit!

Iron Grunty

The Iron Grunty is an excellent friend to trade with before going off to battle Skeith or the Parasite Dragon aboard the Aerial Fleet. Trade for the **Master's Axe** for Piros and the **Flame Sword** for BlackRose.

ATTRIBUTE REQUIRED	RATING
Size	30
Body Odor	3 to 17
Rebel	-2 to 12
Brutality	13 to 27
Intelligence	8 to 22
Purity	-2 to 12

Iron Grunty
Oh master! Thank you so much!
Thanks to you I'm fully grown
clang!

A GOLDEN MEAL

Since the Golden Egg only affects the size rating of the Grunty, Kite can feed the Grunty numerous Golden Eggs to "lock" the other attribute's ratings once they are in accordance with the above requirements.

ITEMS LIST

This section of the book provides a thorough listing of every item that can be acquired in the game. The various items have been split into separate tables corresponding to the selections in Kite's Personal Menu. Those items listed as having an "Attack" or "Weaken" effect can only be used against enemies, whereas those with "Recover" or "Strengthen" properties can only be used on Kite and his allies.

TABLES EXPLAINED

Name	Item name.
Buy	Purchase price if item can be purchased in a shop.
Sell	Price of an item when sold to a shop.
Spell Level	The level and variety of magic.
Effect	The item's effect when used.
Element	The element the item is aligned with.
Target	Whether or not the item targets a unit or a area.
Obtained	How to acquire item: S (Shop), C (Chest or breakable item), T (Trade), E (Event)

ITEMS

NAME	BUY	SELL	EFFECT	OBTAINED
Health Drink	100	50	Restores 150 HP	S/C/T
Healing Potion	N/A	250	Restores 400 HP	C/T
Healing Elixir	N/A	1000	Restores full HP	C/T
Antidote	50	25	Cures Poison, Paralysis, Slow, and Physical Ability Down	S/C/T
Restorative	50	25	Cures Curse, Sleep, Confuse, Charm, and Magical Ability Down	S/C/T
Resurrect	300	150	Revives dead ally	S/C/T
Warrior Blood	100	50	Temporarily increases target's Physical Attack Power	S/C/T
Knight Blood	100	50	Temporarily increases target's Physical Defense Power	S/C/T
Hunter Blood	100	50	Temporarily increases target's Physical Accuracy	S/C/T
Hermit Blood	100	50	Temporarily increases target's Magical Attack Power	S/C/T
Beast Blood	100	50	Temporarily increases target's Magical Defense Power	S/C/T
Wizard's Blood	100	50	Temporarily increases target's Magical Accuracy	S/C/T
Well Water	N/A	50	Temporarily increases target's Earth Attribute	C/T
Pure Water	N/A	50	Temporarily increases target's Water Attribute	C/T
Burning Oil	N/A	50	Temporarily increases target's Fire Attribute	C/T
Holy Sap	N/A	50	Temporarily increases target's Wood Attribute	C/T
Sports Drink	N/A	50	Temporarily increases target's Thunder Attribute	C/T
Cooked Bile	N/A	50	Temporarily increases target's Darkness Attribute	C/T
Mage's Soul	500	250	Restores 100 SP	S/C/T
Artisan's Soul	N/A	1250	Restores 500 SP	C/T
Emperor's Soul	N/A	5000	Restores full SP	T
Noble Wine	N/A	25000	Restores full HP & SP	T
Fortune Wire	10	5	Unlocks booby-trapped treasure boxes	S/C/T
Sprite Ocarina	100	50	Return instantly from dungeon back to the Field	S/C/T
Fairy's Orb	100	50	Unknown parts of Map are displayed	S/C/T

01001010101001100100100100101100

SCROLLS

Name	Buy	Sell	Spell Level	Element	Target	Obtained
Attack Magic Scrolls						
Raining Rocks	200	100	Level 1 Falling	Earth	Area	S/C/T
Stone Storm	N/A	250	Level 2 Falling	Earth	Area	C/T
Meteor Strike	N/A	500	Level 3 Falling	Earth	Area	C/T
Lightning Bolt	200	100	Level 1 Falling	Thunder	Area	S/C/T
Ion Strike	N/A	250	Level 2 Falling	Thunder	Area	C/T
Thunderbolt	N/A	500	Level 3 Falling	Thunder	Area	C/T
Raging Earth	200	100	Level 1 Raising	Earth	Area	S/C/T
Gaia's Spell	N/A	250	Level 2 Raising	Earth	Area	C/T
Cosmic Truth	N/A	500	Level 3 Raising	Earth	Area	C/T
Gale Breath	200	100	Level 1 Raising	Wood	Area	S/C/T
Wood Sprite	N/A	250	Level 2 Raising	Wood	Area	C/T
Forest of Fear	N/A	500	Level 3 Raising	Wood	Area	C/T
Dark Night	200	100	Level 1 Raising	Darkness	Area	S/C/T
Chaos Spell	N/A	250	Level 2 Raising	Darkness	Area	C/T
Nightshade	N/A	500	Level 3 Raising	Darkness	Area	C/T
Ice Storm	200	100	Level 1 Whirlwind	Water	Area	S/C/T
Ice Strike	N/A	250	Level 2 Whirlwind	Water	Area	C/T
Absolute Zero	N/A	500	Level 3 Whirlwind	Water	Area	C/T
Fire Tempest	200	100	Level 1 Whirlwind	Fire	Area	S/C/T
Flame Blast	N/A	250	Level 2 Whirlwind	Fire	Area	C/T
Hellstorm	N/A	500	Level 3 Whirlwind	Fire	Area	C/T
Green Gale	200	100	Level 1 Whirlwind	Wood	Area	S/C/T
Leafblight	N/A	250	Level 2 Whirlwind	Wood	Area	C/T
Jungle Rage	N/A	500	Level 3 Whirlwind	Wood	Area	C/T
Plasma Storm	200	100	Level 1 Whirlwind	Thunder	Area	S/C/T
Raging Plasma	N/A	250	Level 2 Whirlwind	Thunder	Area	C/T
Plasma Gale	N/A	500	Level 3 Whirlwind	Thunder	Area	C/T
Ice Floe	200	100	Level 1 Convergence	Water	Unit	S/C/T
Cygnus	N/A	250	Level 2 Convergence	Water	Unit	C/T
Permafrost	N/A	500	Level 3 Convergence	Water	Unit	C/T
Meteor Swarm	200	100	Level 1 Convergence	Fire	Unit	S/C/T
Fireball Storm	N/A	250	Level 2 Convergence	Fire	Unit	C/T
Inferno Strike	N/A	500	Level 3 Convergence	Fire	Unit	C/T
Nightblight	200	100	Level 1 Convergence	Darkness	Unit	S/C/T
Dark Traitor	N/A	250	Level 2 Convergence	Darkness	Unit	C/T
Nightfear	N/A	500	Level 3 Convergence	Darkness	Unit	C/T

ADDITIONAL ELEMENTS

RAISING
A GRUNTY

ADDITIONAL
ELEMENTS

TRADE
LIST

BOOKS
OF RYU

BESTIARY

MISCELLANEOUS SCROLLS

Name	Buy	Sell	Effect	Obtained
The Death	N/A	100	Poison; HP decreases over time	C/T
The Hanged Man	N/A	100	Paralysis; becomes unable to act	C/T
The Lovers	N/A	100	Charm; may attack allies	C/T
The Moon	N/A	100	Sleep; becomes unable to act	C/T
The Fool	N/A	100	Confuse; attacks friend and foe alike	C/T
The Devil	N/A	100	Curse; SP decreases as time passes	C/T
Warrior's Bane	N/A	100	Target's Physical Attack reduced	C/T
Knight's Bane	N/A	100	Target's Physical Defense reduced	C/T
Hunter's Bane	N/A	100	Target's Physical Accuracy reduced	C/T
Hermit's Bane	N/A	100	Target's Magical Attack reduced	C/T
Beast's Bane	N/A	100	Target's Magical Defense reduced	C/T
Wizard's Bane	N/A	100	Target's Magical Accuracy reduced	C/T
Stonebane	N/A	100	Target's Earth Attribute reduced	C/T
Waterbane	N/A	100	Target's Water Attribute reduced	C/T
Firebane	N/A	100	Target's Fire Attribute reduced	C/T
Treebane	N/A	100	Target's Wood Attribute reduced	C/T
Lightbane	N/A	100	Target's Thunder Attribute reduced	C/T
Nightbane	N/A	100	Target's Darkness Attribute reduced	C/T
Health Charm	N/A	150	HP restored as time passes	C/T
Soul Charm	N/A	300	SP restored as time passes	C/T
Speed Charm	100	50	Moving speed temporarily increases	C/T
Light Cross	1000	500	Restores 150 HP to target and nearby allies	S/C/T
Hale Cross	N/A	1000	Restores 400 HP to target and nearby allies	C/T
Divine Cross	N/A	2500	Restores full HP to target and nearby allies	C/T

BOOKS

Name	Buy	Sell	Effect	Obtained
Power Book	N/A	500	Physical Attack changes permanently by +1	C/T
Tolerance Book	N/A	500	Physical Defense changes permanently by +1	C/T
Insight Book	N/A	500	Magical Attack changes permanently by +1	C/T
Spiritual Book	N/A	500	Magical Defense changes permanently by +1	C/T
Graceful Book	N/A	500	Physical Accuracy changes permanently by +1	C/T
Swift Book	N/A	500	Physical Evasion changes permanently by +1	C/T
Feng Shui	N/A	500	Earth Attribute changes permanently by +1	T
Water Magic	N/A	500	Water Attribute changes permanently by +1	T
Fire Magic	N/A	500	Fire Attribute changes permanently by +1	T
Wood Magic	N/A	500	Wood Attribute changes permanently by +1	T
Thunder Magic	N/A	500	Thunder Attribute changes permanently by +1	T
Black Magic	N/A	500	Darkness Attribute changes permanently by +1	T
Piros's Diary	N/A	50	Magical Attack changes permanently by -1	E

TREASURES

Name	Buy	Sell	Effect	Obtained
Grunty Doll	N/A	250	Can be cashed in for a large sum	C/T
Rainbow Card	N/A	500	Can be cashed in for a large sum	C/T
Yellow Candy	N/A	1000	Can be cashed in for a large sum	C/T
Silver Scarab	N/A	1500	Can be cashed in for a large sum	C/T
Aromatic Grass	N/A	5	Useful in trade	T
Popsicle Stick	N/A	50	Useful in trade	C

0101001010100110010010010010011000

SKILLS LIST

This section of the book provides a thorough listing of each of the Skills that can be used by equipping various weapons and armor. The Skills have been split into separate sections corresponding to the selections in Kite's Personal Menu. Physical Attack Skills have been subdivided based on the type of weapons they are associated with, while Magical Attack Skills have been grouped by their element.

TABLES EXPLAINED

Name	Skill name.
Level	Skill level.
Element	Element associated with Skill.
Target	The area of attack or effect.
AP	Attack Power.
AC	Accuracy Rate.
SP	Skill Points required to use Skill.
Notes	Pertinent information, such as associated weapons class and magical effects.

PHYSICAL ATTACK SKILLS

NAME	LEVEL	ELEMENT	TARGET	AP	AC	SP	NOTES
Saber Dance	1	None	Unit	6	5	10	Twin Blade
Tiger Claws	1	None	Area	6	0	10	Twin Blade
Staccato	1	None	Unit	6	-5	15	Twin Blade
Flame Dance	2	Fire	Unit	6	5	30	Twin Blade
Orchid Dance	2	Wood	Unit	6	5	30	Twin Blade
Thunder Dance	2	Thunder	Unit	6	5	30	Twin Blade
Dark Dance	2	Dark	Unit	6	5	30	Twin Blade
Twin Darkness	2	Dark	Unit	6	-10	45	Twin Blade
Cross Slash	1	None	Unit	6	5	10	Heavy Blade
Crack Beat	1	None	Area	6	0	10	Heavy Blade
Revolver	1	None	Area	6	-5	10	Heavy Blade
Vak Crack	2	Fire	Area	7	10	30	Heavy Blade
Vak Revolver	2	Fire	Area	7	-5	30	Heavy Blade
Ani Slash	2	Dark	Unit	7	0	30	Heavy Blade
Ani Revolver	2	Dark	Area	7	-5	30	Heavy Blade
Death Bringer	1	None	Unit	6	20	10	Heavy Blade
Calamity	1	None	Unit	6	-5	10	Heavy Blade
Gan Smash	2	Earth	Unit	7	20	30	Heavy Blade
Gan Drive	2	Earth	Unit	7	-5	30	Heavy Blade
Vak Smash	2	Fire	Unit	7	20	30	Heavy Blade
Vak Drive	2	Fire	Unit	7	-5	30	Heavy Blade
Juk Smash	2	Wood	Unit	7	20	30	Heavy Blade
Juk Drive	2	Wood	Unit	7	-5	30	Heavy Blade
Rairaku	2	Thunder	Unit	7	20	30	Heavy Blade
Hayabusa	1	None	Area	6	0	10	Blademaster
Sohgasho	1	None	Unit	6	-5	15	Blademaster
Danku	2	Earth	Area	7	0	30	Blademaster
Karin	2	Fire	Area	7	0	30	Blademaster
Hirameki	2	Wood	Area	7	0	30	Blademaster
Raika	2	Thunder	Area	7	0	30	Blademaster
Rairaku	2	Thunder	Unit	7	-5	40	Blademaster
Axel Pain	1	None	Area	6	15	10	Heavy Axeman
Triple Wield	1	None	Area	6	0	10	Heavy Axeman
Brandish	1	None	Area	6	-5	10	Heavy Axeman
Gan Break	2	Earth	Area	7	15	30	Heavy Axeman
Gan Tornado	2	Earth	Area	7	0	30	Heavy Axeman

ADDITIONAL ELEMENTS

PHYSICAL ATTACK SKILLS (CONTINUED)

NAME	LEVEL	ELEMENT	TARGET	AP	AC	SP	NOTES
Gan Basher	2	Earth	Area	7	-5	30	Heavy Axeman
Rue Tornado	2	Water	Area	7	0	30	Heavy Axeman
Rai Tornado	2	Thunder	Area	7	0	30	Heavy Axeman
Rai Basher	2	Thunder	Area	7	-5	30	Heavy Axeman
Ani Tornado	2	Dark	Area	7	0	30	Heavy Axeman
Ani Basher	2	Dark	Area	7	-5	30	Heavy Axeman
Triple Doom	1	None	Unit	6	0	10	Long Arm
Juk Repulse	1	None	Area	6	-5	10	Long Arm
Double Sweep	1	None	Area	6	0	10	Long Arm
Rue Repulse	2	Water	Area	7	-5	30	Long Arm
Vak Repulse	2	Fire	Area	7	-5	30	Long Arm
Juk Wipe	2	Wood	Area	7	0	30	Long Arm
Rai Repulse	2	Thunder	Area	7	-5	30	Long Arm

MAGICAL ATTACK SKILLS

NAME	LEVEL	ELEMENT	TARGET	AP	AC	SP	NOTES
Gan Don	1	Earth	Area	6	20	10	Drop
GiGan Don	2	Earth	Area	8	20	20	Drop
OrGan Don	3	Earth	Area	10	20	40	Drop
Gan Rom	1	Earth	Area	5	10	10	Tornado
MeGan Rom	2	Earth	Area	6	10	20	Tornado
Gan Zot	1	Earth	Area	7	15	20	Raise
GiGan Zot	2	Earth	Area	9	15	30	Raise
OrGan Zot	3	Earth	Area	11	15	50	Raise
Yarthkins	1	Earth	Area	10	99	50	Summon
Rue Rom	1	Water	Area	5	10	10	Tornado
MeRue Rom	2	Water	Area	6	10	20	Tornado
OrRue Rom	3	Water	Area	7	10	40	Tornado
Rue Kruz	1	Water	Unit	8	30	10	Converge
GiRue Kruz	2	Water	Unit	10	30	20	Converge
MeRue Kruz	3	Water	Unit	12	30	40	Converge
Rue Zot	1	Water	Area	7	15	20	Raise
MeRue Zot	2	Water	Area	9	15	30	Raise
Vak Don	1	Fire	Area	6	20	10	Drop
Vak Rom	1	Fire	Area	5	10	10	Tornado
BiVak Rom	2	Fire	Area	6	10	20	Tornado
OrVak Rom	3	Fire	Area	7	10	40	Tornado
Vak Kruz	1	Fire	Unit	8	30	10	Converge
GiVak Kruz	2	Fire	Unit	10	30	20	Converge
MeVak Kruz	3	Fire	Unit	12	30	40	Converge
Vulcan Ch	2	Fire	Area	20	99	70	Summon
Juk Rom	1	Wood	Area	5	10	10	Tornado
ViJuk Rom	2	Wood	Area	6	10	20	Tornado
RaJuk Rom	3	Wood	Area	7	10	40	Tornado
Juk Kruz	1	Wood	Unit	8	30	10	Converge
MeJuk Kruz	2	Wood	Unit	10	30	20	Converge
Juk Zot	1	Wood	Area	7	15	20	Raise
RaJuk Zot	2	Wood	Area	9	15	30	Raise
OrJuk Zot	3	Wood	Area	11	15	50	Raise

MAGICAL ATTACK SKILLS (CONTINUED)

NAME	LEVEL	ELEMENT	TARGET	AP	AC	SP	NOTES
Rai Don	1	Thunder	Area	6	20	10	Drop
MeRai Don	2	Thunder	Area	8	20	20	Drop
GiRai Don	3	Thunder	Area	10	20	40	Drop
Rai Rom	1	Thunder	Area	5	10	10	Tornado
GiRai Rom	2	Thunder	Area	6	10	20	Tornado
MeRai Rom	3	Thunder	Area	7	10	40	Tornado
Rai Kruz	1	Thunder	Unit	8	30	10	Converge
Ani Don	1	Dark	Area	6	20	10	Drop
Ani Kruz	1	Dark	Unit	8	30	10	Converge
MeAni Kruz	2	Dark	Unit	10	30	20	Converge
OrmeAni Kruz	3	Dark	Unit	12	30	40	Converge
Ani Zot	1	Dark	Area	7	15	20	Raise
MeAni Zot	2	Dark	Area	9	15	30	Raise
OrmeAni Zot	3	Dark	Area	11	15	50	Raise
Wryneck	1	Dark	Area	10	99	50	Summon
Summon Goblin	1	None	Area	10	99	25	Summon

RECOVER SKILLS

NAME	LEVEL	ELEMENT	TARGET	AP	AC	SP	NOTES
Repth	1	None	Unit	0	5	10	Restores 150 HP.
Ol Repth	2	None	Unit	0	5	30	Restores 400 HP.
Pha Repth	3	None	Unit	0	5	50	Restores all HP.
La Repth	1	None	Area	0	5	20	Restores 150 HP to target and surrounding allies.
Ola Repth	2	None	Area	0	5	40	Restores 400 HP to target and surrounding allies.
Phal Repth	3	None	Area	0	5	60	Restores all HP to target and surrounding allies.
Rip Teyn	1	None	Unit	0	5	10	Cures Poison, Paralysis, Slow, and Downs on Physical abilities.
Rip Synk	1	None	Unit	0	5	10	Cures Curse, Sleep, Confuse, Charm, and Downs on Magical abilities.
Rip Maen	1	None	Unit	0	5	40	Returns Ghosted allies back to life.

01001101010010101010101001001

STRENGTHENING SKILLS

Name	Level	Element	Target	AP	AC	SP	Notes
Rig Saem	1	None	Unit	0	5	15	HP replenishes for a set time.
Rig Geam	1	None	Unit	0	5	25	SP replenishes for a set time.
Ap Do	1	None	Unit	0	5	15	Temporarily ups Movement Speed.
Ap Corv	1	None	Unit	5	5	15	Temporarily ups Physical Attack.
Ap Vorv	1	None	Unit	5	5	15	Temporarily ups Physical Defense.
Ap Torv	1	None	Unit	0	15	15	Temporarily ups Physical Accuracy.
Ap Corma	1	None	Unit	5	5	15	Temporarily ups Magical Attack.
Ap Vorma	1	None	Unit	5	5	15	Temporarily ups Magical Defense.
Ap Torma	1	None	Unit	0	15	15	Temporarily ups Magical Accuracy.
Ap Ganz	1	Earth	Area	0	5	10	Temporarily ups target and surrounding allies' Earth attribute.
Ap Ruem	1	Water	Area	0	5	10	Temporarily ups target and surrounding allies' Water attribute.
Ap Vakz	1	Fire	Area	0	5	10	Temporarily ups target and surrounding allies' Fire attribute.
Ap Juka	1	Wood	Area	0	5	10	Temporarily ups target and surrounding allies' Wood attribute.
Ap Raio	1	Thunder	Area	0	5	10	Temporarily ups target and surrounding allies' Thunder attribute.
Ap Anid	1	Dark	Area	0	5	10	Temporarily ups target and surrounding allies' Dark attribute.

WEAKENING SKILLS

Name	Level	Element	Target	AP	AC	SP	Notes
Duk Lei	1	None	Unit	0	5	20	Poisons enemy for a set time.
Suvi Lei	1	None	Unit	0	5	20	Paralyzes enemy for a set time.
Dek Do	1	None	Unit	0	5	20	Slows enemy for a set time.
Miu Lei	1	None	Unit	0	5	40	Charms enemy for a set time.
Mumyn Lei	1	None	Unit	0	5	30	Sleeps enemy for a set time.
Ranki Lei	1	None	Unit	0	5	30	Confuses enemy for a set time.
Maj Lei	1	None	Unit	0	5	30	Curses enemy for a set time.
Dek Corv	1	None	Unit	-10	5	15	Temporarily drops enemy's Physical Attack.
Dek Vorv	1	None	Unit	-10	5	15	Temporarily drops enemy's Physical Defense.
Dek Torv	1	None	Unit	0	-20	15	Temporarily drops enemy's Physical Accuracy.
Dek Corma	1	None	Unit	-10	5	15	Temporarily drops enemy's Magical Attack.
Dek Vorma	1	None	Unit	-10	5	15	Temporarily drops enemy's Magical Defense.
Dek Torma	1	None	Unit	0	-20	15	Temporarily drops enemy's Magical Accuracy.
Dek Ganz	1	Earth	Area	0	5	10	Temporarily drops target and surrounding enemies' Earth attribute.
Dek Ruem	1	Water	Area	0	5	10	Temporarily drops target and surrounding enemies' Water attribute.
Dek Vakz	1	Fire	Area	0	5	10	Temporarily drops target and surrounding enemies' Fire attribute.
Dek Juka	1	Wood	Area	0	5	10	Temporarily drops target and surrounding enemies' Wood attribute.
Dek Raio	1	Thunder	Area	0	5	10	Temporarily drops target and surrounding enemies' Thunder attribute.
Dek Anid	1	Dark	Area	0	5	10	Temporarily drops target and surrounding enemies' Dark attribute.

DATA DRAIN

Name	Level	Element	Target	AP	AC	SP	Notes
Data Drain	1	None	Unit	0	0	10	Absorbs enemy data, thereby dropping its level.

| Dark History | 14* | -/2150 | 0/22 | 0/25 | 0/0 | 3 | 3 | 3 | 3 | 3 | 3 | -/- | Rue Rom, MeRue Zot |
| Jester's Wand | 14* | -/2100 | 0/25 | 0/10 | -15/0 | 3 | 3 | 3 | 3 | 3 | 3 | -/- | Rai Don, GiRai Rom |

Heavy Axeman Class

Armor

Heavy Armor

Not all armor can be worn by all class types. Armor noted as "Type A" means that the piece of equipment can't be used by a Wavemaster. Armor designated as "Type B" can't be worn by a Twin Blade, Long Arm, or Wavemaster.

Head

Name	Lv	B/S	P/M Atk	P/M Acc	P/M Evd	Earth	Water	Fire	Wood	Thunder	Darkness	M/B Res	Skills	Notes
Bandana	1	-/200	0/2	0/0	0/6	1	1	1	1	1	1	4/0	Repth	
Nomad's Hood	2	-/250	1/1	0/0	1/1	1	1	1	1	1	1	0/0	Repth	Type A
Head Gear	3	-/300	2/0	0/0	6/0	1	1	1	1	1	1	0/4	Ap Ganz	Type B
Time Headband	4*	-/350	0/0	0/0	25/0	0	0	0	0	0	0	0/0	Ap Do	
Steel Cap	6	800/400	0/3	0/0	0/7	1	1	1	1	1	1	5/0	Repth	
Goblin Cap	6*	-/400	1/0	0/0	0/0	0	0	0	0	0	0	0/20	Maj Lei	Type A
Guard Cap	7	900/450	1/1	0/0	2/2	1	1	1	1	1	1	0/0	Repth	Type A
Ceramic Helm	7*	-/450	2/5	0/0	3/5	1	1	1	1	1	1	1/2	N/A	Type B
Face Guard	8	1000/500	3/0	0/0	7/0	1	1	1	1	1	1	0/5	Ap Ruem	Type B
Cougar Bandana	11	-/600	0/3	0/0	0/8	1	1	1	1	1	1	6/0	La Repth	
Hunter's Hood	12	-/650	2/2	0/0	3/3	4	1	1	1	1	1	1/1	Repth	Type A
Mountain Helm	13	-/700	3/0	0/0	8/0	1	1	1	1	1	1	0/6	Ap Ganz	Type B
Racoon Earcap	16	-/800	0/3	0/0	0/9	2	4	0	2	2	2	7/0	La Repth	
Ice Hunter Hat	17	-/850	2/2	0/0	4/4	2	4	0	2	2	2	2/2	Repth	Type A
Ice Helm	18	-/900	3/0	0/0	9/0	2	4	0	2	2	2	0/7	Ap Ruem	Type B
Newt Necklace	21	-/1000	0/3	0/0	0/10	2	0	4	2	2	2	8/0	La Repth	
Fire Dance Hat	22	-/1050	2/2	0/0	5/5	2	0	4	2	2	2	3/3	Repth	Type A
Fire Helm	23	-/1100	3/0	0/0	10/0	2	0	4	2	2	2	0/8	Ap Vakz	Type B
Scarab Earring	26	-/-	0/3	0/0	0/11	0	2	2	4	2	2	9/0	La Repth, Rip Maen	
Peasant's Hat	27	-/1250	2/2	0/0	6/6	0	2	2	4	2	2	4/4	Repth, Rip Teyn	Type A
Forester Helm	28	-/1300	3/0	0/0	11/0	0	2	2	4	2	2	0/9	Ap Juka, Ap Vorma	Type B
Thunder Torque	31	-/1400	0/3	0/0	0/12	2	2	2	2	4	0	10/0	La Repth, Rip Maen	
Lightning Cap	32	-/1450	2/2	0/0	7/7	2	2	2	2	4	0	5/5	Repth, Rip Synk	Type A
Stormlord Helm	33	-/1500	3/0	0/0	12/0	2	2	2	2	4	0	0/10	Ap Torv, Ap Raio	Type B

Body

Name	Lv	B/S	P/M Atk	P/M Acc	P/M Evd	Earth	Water	Fire	Wood	Thunder	Darkness	M/B Res	Skills	Notes
Leather Coat	1	-/200	0/2	0/0	0/6	1	1	1	1	1	1	4/0	Gan Zot	
Leather Armor	2	-/250	1/1	0/0	1/1	1	1	1	1	1	1	0/0	Vak Kruz	Type A
Brigandine	3	-/300	2/0	0/0	6/0	1	1	1	1	1	1	0/4	N/A	Type B
Time Sash	4*	-/350	0/0	0/0	0/25	0	0	0	0	0	0	0/0	Ap Do	
Noble Cloak	6	-/400	0/3	0/0	0/7	1	1	1	1	1	1	5/0	Rue Zot	
Goblin Mail	6*	-/400	1/0	0/0	0/0	0	0	0	0	0	0	0/20	Dek Do	Type A
Ring Mail	7	-/450	1/1	0/0	2/2	1	1	1	1	1	1	0/0	Juk Kruz	Type A
Kagayuzen	8*	-/500	0/8	0/10	0/8	0	0	0	0	0	0	8/0	Miu Lei	Magical Attack +10
Plate Armor	8	-/500	3/0	0/0	7/0	1	1	1	1	1	1	0/5	N/A	Type B
Hiking Gear	11	1200/600	0/3	0/0	0/8	1	1	1	1	1	1	6/0	Gan Zot	
Wyrm Hide	12	1300/650	2/2	0/0	3/3	4	2	2	0	2	2	1/1	Gan Don	Type A
Grand Armor	13	1400/700	3/0	0/0	8/0	4	2	2	0	2	2	0/6	Ap Ganz	Type B
Winter Coat	16	-/800	0/3	0/0	0/9	2	4	0	2	2	2	7/0	Rue Zot	
Wyrm Scale	17	-/850	2/2	0/0	4/4	2	4	0	2	2	2	2/2	Rue Kruz	Type A
Frost Armor	18	-/900	3/0	0/0	9/0	2	4	0	2	2	2	0/7	Ap Ruem	Type B
Fireman's Coat	21	-/1000	0/3	0/0	0/10	2	0	4	2	2	2	8/0	Vak Kruz	
Firedrake Mail	22	-/1050	2/2	0/0	5/5	2	0	4	2	2	2	3/3	Vak Kruz	Type A
Blaze Armor	23	-/1100	4/1	0/0	10/1	2	0	4	2	2	2	0/8	Ap Vakz	Type B
Lincoln Green	26	-/1200	0/3	0/0	0/11	0	2	2	4	2	2	9/0	Juk Zot	
Holy Tree Mail	27	-/1250	2/2	0/0	6/6	0	2	2	4	2	2	4/4	Juk Kruz	Type A
Spirit Armor	28	-/1300	3/0	0/0	11/0	0	2	2	4	2	2	0/9	Ap Juka	Type B
Thunder Cloak	31	-/1400	0/3	0/0	0/12	2	2	2	2	4	0	10/0	Rai Kruz	
Quakebeast Fur	32	-/1450	2/2	0/0	7/7	2	2	2	2	4	0	5/5	Rai Kruz	Type A
Thunder Armor	33	-/1500	3/0	0/0	12/0	2	2	2	2	4	0	0/10	Ap Raio	Type B

HANDS

Name	Lv	B/S	P/M Atk	P/M Acc	P/M Evd	Earth	Water	Fire	Wood	Thunder	Darkness	M/B Res	Skills	Notes
Wrist Band	1	-/200	0/2	0/0	0/6	1	1	1	1	1	1	4/0	Juk Rom	
Leather Gloves	2	-/250	1/1	0/0	1/1	1	1	1	1	1	1	0/0	N/A	Type A
Rusted Hands	3	-/300	2/0	0/0	6/0	1	1	1	1	1	1	0/4	N/A	Type B
Time Bracer	4*	-/350	0/0	0/0	25/0	0	0	0	0	0	0	0/0	Ap Do	
Silver Bracer	6	800/400	0/3	0/0	0/7	1	1	1	1	1	1	5/0	Rai Rom	
Goblin Gloves	6*	-/400	1/0	0/0	0/0	0	0	0	0	0	0	0/20	Maj Lei	Type A
Silver Gloves	7	900/450	1/1	0/0	2/2	1	1	1	1	1	1	0/0	N/A	Type A
Silver Hands	8	1000/500	3/0	0/0	7/0	1	1	1	1	1	1	0/5	N/A	Type B
Fossil Bracer	11	-/600	0/3	0/0	0/8	4	2	2	0	2	2	6/0	Gan Rom	
Miner's Gloves	12	-/650	2/2	0/0	3/3	4	1	1	1	1	1	1/1	Gan Don	Type A
Hands of Earth	13	-/700	3/0	0/0	8/0	4	2	2	0	2	2	0/6	Dek Ganz	Type B
Frost Bracer	16	-/800	0/3	0/0	0/9	2	4	0	2	2	2	7/0	Rue Rom	
Fishing Gloves	17	-/850	2/2	0/0	4/4	2	4	0	2	2	2	2/2	Rue Kruz	Type A
Hands of Water	18	-/900	3/0	0/0	9/0	2	4	0	2	2	2	0/7	Dek Ruem	Type B
Fire Bracer	21	-/1000	0/3	0/0	0/10	2	0	4	2	2	2	8/0	Vak Rom	
Smith's Gloves	22	-/1050	2/2	0/0	5/5	2	0	4	2	2	2	3/3	Vak Don	Type A
Hands of Fire	23	-/1100	4/1	0/0	10/1	2	0	4	2	2	2	0/8	Dek Vakz	Type B
Air Bracer	27	-/1250	2/2	0/0	6/6	0	2	2	4	2	2	4/4	Dek Juka	Type A
Hands of Wood	28	-/1300	3/0	0/0	11/0	0	2	2	4	2	2	0/9	Dek Juka	Type B
Storm Bracer	31	-/1400	0/3	0/0	0/12	2	2	2	2	4	0	10/0	Rue Rom	
Thunder Gloves	32	-/1450	2/2	0/0	7/7	2	2	2	2	4	0	5/5	Dek Raio	Type A
Hands of Storm	33	-/1500	3/0	0/0	12/0	2	2	2	2	4	0	0/10	Dek Raio	Type B

LEGS/FEET

Name	Lv	B/S	P/M Atk	P/M Acc	P/M Evd	Earth	Water	Fire	Wood	Thunder	Darkness	M/B Res	Skills	Notes
Sandals	1	-/200	0/2	0/0	0/6	1	1	1	1	1	1	4/0	N/A	
Safety Shoes	2	-/250	1/1	0/0	1/1	1	1	1	1	1	1	0/0	N/A	Type A
Used Greaves	3	-/300	2/0	0/0	6/0	1	1	1	1	1	1	0/4	N/A	Type B
Time Sandals	4*	-/350	0/0	0/0	0/25	0	0	0	0	0	0	0/0	Ap Do	
Leg Mail	6	-/400	0/3	0/0	0/7	1	1	1	1	1	1	5/0	N/A	
Jungle Boots	7	-/450	1/1	0/0	2/2	1	1	1	1	1	1	0/0	N/A	Type A
Leather Legs	8	-/500	3/0	0/0	7/0	1	1	1	1	1	1	0/5	N/A	Type B
Goblin Boots	9*	-/150	3/4	0/2	0/9	0	0	0	0	0	0	0/20	Dek Juka	Type A
Ceramic Anklet	11	1200/600	0/3	0/0	0/8	4	2	2	0	2	2	6/0	Dek Ganz	
Mountain Boots	12	1300/650	2/2	0/0	3/3	4	1	1	1	1	1	1/1	Ap Corv	Type A
Mountain Guard	13	1400/700	3/0	0/0	8/0	4	2	2	0	2	2	0/6	Repth	Type B
Frost Anklet	16	-/800	0/3	0/0	0/9	2	4	0	2	2	2	7/0	Dek Ruem	
Snow Panther	17	-/850	2/2	0/0	4/4	2	4	0	2	2	2	2/2	Ap Vorv	Type A
Aqua Guard	18	-/900	3/0	0/0	9/0	2	4	0	2	2	2	0/7	Rip Teyn	Type B
Iron Anklet	21	-/1000	0/3	0/0	0/10	2	0	4	2	2	2	8/0	Dek Vakz	
Fire Lizard	22	-/1050	2/2	0/0	5/5	2	0	4	2	2	2	3/3	Ap Torv	Type A
Flare Guard	23	-/1100	4/1	0/0	10/1	2	0	4	2	2	2	0/8	Rip Synk	Type B
Oak Anklet	26	-/1200	0/3	0/0	0/11	0	2	2	4	2	2	9/0	Dek Juka	
Ranger's Boots	27	-/1250	2/2	0/0	6/6	0	2	2	4	2	2	4/4	Ap Corma	Type A
Green Guards	28	-/1300	3/0	0/0	11/0	0	2	2	4	2	2	0/9	Rig Saem	Type B
Thunder Anklet	31	-/1400	0/3	0/0	0/12	2	2	2	2	4	0	10/0	Dek Raio	
Thunder Boots	32	-/1450	2/2	0/0	7/7	2	2	2	2	4	0	5/5	Ap Vorma	Type A
Electric Guard	33	-/1500	5/2	0/0	11/1	2	2	2	2	4	0	0/10	Repth	Type B

TRADE LIST

Kite can trade with each of the other player characters (PCs) in "The World," including those who become his friends. Some of the players will suggest very specific trades for valuable items, whereas many others are open for any number of offers. It's also important to succeed in raising a Grunty to a full-grown Adult Grunty. When done correctly, Kite can trade it for rare and, oftentimes, powerful weapons. Read the section on trading in the "Advanced Hacking" chapter.

NEVER ENDING SUPPLIES

Those items marked with an * (asterisk) are automatically replenished and can be traded for numerous times throughout the game.

KITE'S FRIENDS

These characters are willing to give Kite their flash mail address, thereby enabling Kite to invite them to join in his adventures. Kite can trade openly with these characters for weapons that aren't available in shops. Also, as their affection toward Kite increases, he can trade cheaper items for more valuable ones.

NAME	TRADE ITEMS
Orca	Speed Charm*
BlackRose	Speed Charm*
Mia	Speed Charm*, Assassin, Flame Axe, Relief Lance, Plate Armor, The Lovers
Elk	Speed Charm*, Curing Sword, Gakaku, Raging Earth, The Lovers
Mistral	Speed Charm*, Curing Sword, Gakaku, Raging Earth, Spear of Spell, Plate Armor
Piros	Speed Charm*, Grunt Doll, Yellow Candy, Cypress Wand
Natsume	Speed Charm*, Fire Spear
Gardenia	Speed Charm*, Hands of Wood, Health Charm, Hands of Earth
Sanjuro	Speed Charm*, Nihonmaru, Ice Storm, Basho Wand

GRUNTIES

Kite can raise three different Grunties to maturity. By doing so, he'll gain three devoted friends willing to trade valuable items with him. Kite must gather large amounts of Grunty Food from the various areas to meet the dietary requests of the Grunties at the ranch on the Θ server.

NAME	TRADE ITEMS
Iron Grunty	Forester Helm, Ice Helm, Fire Helm, Claymore, Aromatic Grass
Noble Grunty	Grunt Doll*, Rainbow Card*, Yellow Candy*, Silver Scarab, Bloody Blades
Poison Grunty	Fire Tempest*, Stonebane*, Unicorn Blade, Slayer, Midnight Axe

PLAYER CHARACTERS

Kite encounters frequent PCs in each server's Root Town. The majority of them are willing to chat with Kite and even trade away the items in their possession. Trading with these characters for weaponry is the single-best way to gain valuable equipment for both Kite and his friends.

Name	Trade Items
Wing	Health Charm*, Mage's Soul*, Life Sword, Flame Axe, Steel Cap, Spark Blades, Stun Sword, Cougar Bandana, Miner's Gloves, Shidan, Snow Panther
Macky	Soul Charm*, Artisan's Soul*, Assassin, Wind Axe, Cougar Bandana, Lath Blades, Raccoon Earcap, Fishing Gloves, Fireman's Coat, Oak Anklet
NOVA	Speed Charm*, Emperor's Soul*, Hell's Gate, Thunder Axe, Guard Cap, Fuse Blades, Nodachi, Newt Necklace, Smith's Gloves, Iron Anklet, Frost Anklet
Sachiko	Light Cross*, Noble Wine*, Amateur Blades, Fire Spear, Hunter's Hood, Shadow Blades, Stun Sword, Mountain Helm, Smith's Gloves, Earth Rod
Neja	Hale Cross*, Forest of Fear*, Life Sword, Wooden Spear, Face Guard, Slayer, Ice Hunter Hat, Ice Helm, Shanato
Heavy	Divine Cross*, Lightning Bolt*, Assassin, Electric Spear, Mountain Helm, Lath Blades, Nodachi, Fire Dance Hat, Fire Helm, Fossil Bracer, Magnifier
Benkei	Warrior Blood*, Plasma Storm*, Hell's Gate, Earth Wand, Noble Cloak, Stun Sword, Mountain Helm, Mountain Boots, Enou
Hayate	Knight Blood*, Ion Strike*, Amateur Blades, Water Wand, Hiking Gear, Slayer, Ice Helm, Snow Panther, Hands of Water
Task	Hunter Blood*, Raging Plasma*, Gakaku, Fire Wand, Ring Mail, Spark Blades, Nodachi, Fire Helm, Fire Lizard, Byakuen
Hinata	Hermit Blood*, Thunderbolt*, Strange Blade, Earth Wand, Leather Armor, Lath Blades, Stun Sword, Hiking Gear, Hunter's Hood, Raccoon Earcap
A-Kichi	Beast Blood*, Plasma Gale*, Assassin, Water Wand, Plate Armor, Fuse Blades, Slayer, Winter Coat, Ice Hunter Hat, Cedar Wand
Cleama	Wizard Blood*, Nightblight*, Curing Sword, Fire Wand, Grand Armor, Shadow Blades, Nodachi, Fireman's Coat, Fire Dance Hat, Raijin
Grid	Health Drink*, Dark Night*, Life Sword, Silver Bracer, Spark Blades, Fire Wand, Wyrm Hide, Cougar Bandana, Shidan
Quess	Healing Potion*, Dark Traitor*, Green Sword, Assassin, Fossil Bracer, Lath Blades, Air Wand, Wyrm Scale, Earth Rod
Nekoski	Healing Elixir*, Chaos Spell*, Hell's Gate, Rusted Hands, Fuse Blades, Electric Wand, Firedrake Mail, Newt Necklace, Bandit's Axe
Gyokuro	Antidote*, Nightfear*, Curing Sword, Amateur Blades, Miner's Gloves, Shadow Blades, Flame Axe, Grand Armor, Mountain Boots, Shanato
Osugi	Restorative*, Nightshade*, Life Sword, Silver Gloves, Spark Blades, Wind Axe, Frost Armor, Snow Panther, Absorber
Acerola	Resurrect*, The Death*, Green Sword, Assassin, Lath Blades, Thunder Axe, Blaze Armor, Fire Lizard, Lincoln Green
Borscht	Warrior Blood*, The Hanged Man*, Hell's Gate, Leg Mail, Fuse Blades, Flame Axe, Fossil Bracer, Wyrm Hide, Ice Helm
M-78	Knight Blood*, The Lovers*, Flame Axe, Amateur Blades, Ceramic Anklet, Shadow Blades, Frost Bracer, Wyrm Scale, Bloody Lance
Yuckey	Hunter Blood*, The Moon*, Wind Axe, Gakaku, Jungle Boots, Thunder Axe, Firedrake Mail, Lincoln Green
Nijukata	Hermit Blood*, The Fool*, Thunder Axe, Strange Blade, Ranger's Boots, Lath Blades, Fire Spear, Miner's Gloves, Ceramic Anklet, Firedrake Mail
Hirami	Beast Blood*, The Devil*, Fire Spear, Assassin, Leather Legs, Fuse Blades, Wooden Spear, Fishing Gloves, Frost Anklet, Earth Axe
Henako	Wizard Blood*, Warrior's Bane*, Wooden Spear, Curing Sword, Mountain Guard, Shadow Blades, Electric Spear, Smith's Gloves, Cedar Wand
BIG	Ice Floe*, Knight's Bane*, Electric Spear, Spark Blades, Fire Spear, Hands of Earth, Hunter's Hood, Snow Panther
Yuji	Ice Strike*, Hunter's Bane*, Earth Wand, Green Sword, Lath Blades, Wooden Spear, Hands of Water, Ice Hunter Hat, Firedrake Mail
Cima	Cygnus*, Hermit's Bane*, Water Wand, Berserk Spear, Fuse Blades, Electric Spear, Hands of Fire, Fire Dance Hat, Cedar Wand
Koji	Absolute Zero*, Beast's Bane*, Fire Wand, Curing Sword, Raitei, Shadow Blades, Ceramic Anklet, Wyrm Hide, Fire Bracer
Crest	Permafrost*, Wizard's Bane*, Earth Wand, Spark Blades, Frost Anklet, Ice Helm
Mayunosuke	Fire Tempest*, Stonebane*, Water Wand, Green Sword, Electric Wand, Iron Anklet, Ceramic Anklet
Mutsuki	Meteor Swarm*, Waterbane*, Fire Wand, Gakaku, Mountain Boots, Dogman's Sword, Mountain Guard, Treeman Spear
Oborozukiyo	Flame Blast*, Firebane*, Life Sword, Water Wand, Air Wand, Snow Panther, Aqua Guard
Bell	Fireball Storm*, Treebane, Assasin, Fire Wand, Executioner, Electric Wand, Fire Lizard, Flare Guard, Hands of Fire
Cossack Leader	Hellstorm*, Lightbane*, Hell's Gate, Life Sword, Adian's Rod, Silver Bracer, Gakaku, Fire Wand, Mountain Guard, Fishing Gloves, Inferno Wand
Alue	Inferno Strike*, Nightbane*, Amateur Blades, Assassin, Strange Blade, Air Wand, Aqua Guard, Smith's Gloves, Cedar Wand
Alpha Ichigoro	Green Gale*, Health Charm*, Hell's Gate, Executioner, Electric Wand, Flare Guard, Hands of Earth, Bloody Blades

Special Trades

Kite will also encounter 14 PCs who don't respond to typical trade offers. Instead, they have specific trading requirements and will only accept bulk quantities of a particular item (such as Burning Oil or Pure Water). The items they desire can only be obtained in the field or, more commonly, in dungeons.

Name	Trade Item	Req Offer	Trade Item	Req Offer	Trade Item	Req Offer
Alicia	Hands of Earth	Well Water x 10	Fossil Bracer	Well Water x 10	Power Book	Well Water x 25
Stare	Hands of Water	Pure Water x 10	Frost Bracer	Pure Water x 10	Tolerance Book	Pure Water x 25
Flare	Hands of Fire	Burning Oil x 10	Fire Bracer	Burning Oil x 10	Insight Book	Burning Oil x 25
Fool	Hands of Wood	Holy Sap x 10	Air Bracer	Holy Sap x 10	Spiritual Book	Holy Sap x 25
Teria	Hands of Storm	Sports Drink x 10	Storm Bracer	Sports Drink x 10	Graceful Book	Sports Drink x 25
Waffle	Ebony Wand	Cooked Bile x 10	Shadow Blades	Cooked Bile x 10	Swift Book	Cooked Bile x 25
Cyan	Miner's Gloves	Well Water x 10	Ceramic Anklet	Well Water x 10	Feng Shui	Well Water x 25
Panta	Fishing Gloves	Pure Water x 10	Frost Anklet	Pure Water x 10	Water Magic	Pure Water x 25
Jutah	Smith's Gloves	Burning Oil x 10	Iron Anklet	Burning Oil x 10	Fire Magic	Burning Oil x 25
Annri	Air Bracer	Holy Sap x 10	Oak Anklet	Holy Sap x 10	Wood Magic	Holy Sap x 25
Benoit	Thunder Gloves	Sports Drink x 10	Thunder Anklet	Sports Drink x 10	Thunder Magic	Sports Drink x 25
John	Midnight Axe	Cooked Bile x 10	Unicorn Blade	Cooked Bile x 10	Black Magic	Cooked Bile x 25
Micino	Grand Armor	Silver Axe x 5	Hiking Gear	Silver Axe x 5	Thunder Cloak	Golden Axe x 10 and Silver Axe x 10
Tim	Ice Hunter Hat	Golden Axe x 5	Fire Dance Hat	Golden Axe x 5	Thunder Torque	Golden Axe x 10 and Silver Axe x 10

BOOKS OF RYU

There are dozens of unlockable multimedia bonuses to acquire while playing *.hack//INFECTION*. Each of the Ryu Books listed in the Key Items screen can be used to unlock background music (BGM), movies, and images that can all be accessed via the desktop after logging out of "The World." Although you can only view the unlocked movies after completing the game, the images and background music can be used to enhance the look and feel of the desktop at any time. Make a point to periodically inspect each of the Ryu Books for new unlockables.

RYU BOOK SECRETS

Each Ryu Book can only be used a finite number of times to create an item in this volume of the game. Ryu Books will unlock background music, a movie, or an image in an alternating pattern whenever one of the milestones listed below has been reached.

RYU BOOK I

Chronicles the total number of areas and total play time.

PLAY TIME
Over 5:00:00 Total Play Time
Over 10:00:00 Total Play Time
Over 15:00:00 Total Play Time

AREAS VISITED
Over 10 Areas Visited
Over 20 Areas Visited
Over 30 Areas Visited
Over 40 Areas Visited
Over 50 Areas Visited

RYU BOOK II

Chronicles the total number of Magic Portals in the field and dungeons.

MAGIC PORTALS OPENED
Over 50 Magic Portals Opened
Over 100 Magic Portals Opened
Over 150 Magic Portals Opened
Over 200 Magic Portals Opened
Over 300 Magic Portals Opened
Over 400 Magic Portals Opened

FIELDS CLEARED OF MAGIC PORTALS
Over 5 Fields Cleared
Over 10 Fields Cleared

DUNGEONS CLEARED OF MAGIC PORTALS
Over 10 Dungeons Cleared
Over 15 Dungeons Cleared

RYU BOOK III

Chronicles the names of players Kite has met.

PLAYER NAMES
Over 20 Names Registered

TRADES
Over 5 Trades
Over 10 Trades

RYU BOOK IV

Chronicles the names of monsters Kite has fought.

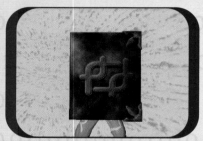

MONSTERS ENCOUNTERED

Over 40 Monsters Listed
Over 80 Monsters Listed

RYU BOOK V

Chronicles about Kite's friends.

GIFT AMOUNT

Over 20,000 GP in Gifts
Over 50,000 GP in Gifts

RYU BOOK VI

Chronicles about Gott Statues, treasures, boxes, casks, jars, and bones.

TREASURE BOXES

Over 50 Treasure Boxes Opened
Over 150 Treasure Boxes Opened
Over 300 Treasure Boxes Opened

CASKS, BOXES, JARS DESTROYED

Over 50 Casks/Boxes/Jars Destroyed
Over 100 Casks/Boxes/Jars Destroyed
Over 200 Casks/Boxes/Jars Destroyed

GOTT STATUE TREASURES

Over 5 Gott Statue Treasures Opened
Over 15 Gott Statue Treasures Opened

RYU BOOK VII

Chronicles about Spring of Myst and Symbols.

SYMBOLS ACTIVATED

Over 5 Symbols Activated
Over 10 Symbols Activated
Over 20 Symbols Activated
Over 30 Symbols Activated

ENCOUNTERS WITH MONSIEUR

Over 5 Encounters with Monsieur
Over 10 Encounters with Monsieur

ENCOUNTERS WITH GRANDPA

Over 5 Encounters with Grandpa
Over 10 Encounters with Grandpa

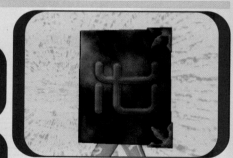

RYU BOOK VIII

Chronicles about Grunties and Food for Grunties.

GRUNTY LIST

No Items Awarded

GRUNTY FOOD

Over 50 Grunty Food Obtained
Obtain All Grunty Food Varieties

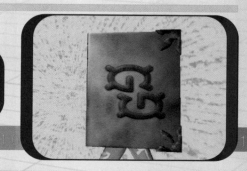

RAISING
A GRUNTY

ADDITIONAL
ELEMENTS

TRADE
LIST

BOOKS
OF RYU

BESTIARY

BESTIARY

This chapter provides a detailed listing of every monster in the game along with its vital information, the skills it uses, and the items that can be obtained by Data Draining it. The main portion of this section deals with the monsters fought in the field and dungeons; it's also important to note that the enemies are listed *by level* for easier reference. To prevent confusion, Drained Monsters, Goblins, and bosses appear separately.

DON'T FORGET...

As noted earlier, the enemies are listed by level. This provides a much easier reference tool to find particular enemies of the same level.

Species	Family of monster to which the creature belongs.
Level	Monster's level.
Size	The size of the enemy dictates which Virus Cores can be obtained by Data Draining it. Small (S) creatures yield Virus Core A, medium (M) creatures yield Virus Core B, and large (L) creatures can yield a Virus Core C.
Data Drain Monster	Name of drained monster that appears after Data Drain is performed.
HP/SP/PP	The monster's Hit Points (HP), Skill Points (SP), and Protect Points (PP). The monster can be Data Drained when reduced to an HP equaling the PP.
Resistance	Level of resistance to attacks against the mind (Curse, Sleep, Confuse, Charm, and Magical Ability Down) and the body (Poison, Paralysis, Speed Down, Physical Ability Down, and Attribute Down).
Physical/Magical	The enemy's Attack (Atk), Defense (Def), Accuracy (Acc), and Evade (Evd) ratings.
Element	The enemy's ratings for Earth, Water, Fire, Wood, Thunder, and Darkness.
Skills	The Skills used by the monster.
Data Drain Items	Items received by Data Draining the creature.

Standard Enemies

GOBLIN — Species: Goblin

LEVEL	1	SIZE	S	DATA DRAIN MONSTER	Gremlin

HP/SP/PP	50/15/16	MIND/BODY RESISTANCE	1.3/2.0

PHYSICAL/MAGICAL ATK	3.1/0.6
PHYSICAL/MAGICAL DEF	3.7/1.7
PHYSICAL/MAGICAL ACC	3.0/1.3
PHYSICAL/MAGICAL EVD	0.4/0.2

EARTH	0.7	WATER	0.1	FIRE	0.1
WOOD	0.0	THUNDER	0.1	DARKNESS	0.1

SKILLS: N/A

DATA DRAIN ITEMS
Steel Blades, Leather Gloves

DISCO KNIFE — Species: Knife

LEVEL	1	SIZE	S	DATA DRAIN MONSTER	Limp Blade

HP/SP/PP	60/25/26	MIND/BODY RESISTANCE	1.3/2.0

PHYSICAL/MAGICAL ATK	3.1/0.6
PHYSICAL/MAGICAL DEF	3.7/1.7
PHYSICAL/MAGICAL ACC	3.0/1.3
PHYSICAL/MAGICAL EVD	0.4/0.2

EARTH	0.1	WATER	0.1	FIRE	0.1
WOOD	0.1	THUNDER	0.1	DARKNESS	0.1

SKILLS: Ap Corv

DATA DRAIN ITEMS
Earth Sword, Bronze Spear, Rondo

MAD GRASS — Species: Plant

LEVEL	1	SIZE	S	DATA DRAIN MONSTER	Sunnyflower

HP/SP/PP	60/15/26	MIND/BODY RESISTANCE	1.3/2.0

PHYSICAL/MAGICAL ATK	3.1/1.0
PHYSICAL/MAGICAL DEF	3.7/1.7
PHYSICAL/MAGICAL ACC	3.0/1.3
PHYSICAL/MAGICAL EVD	0.4/0.4

EARTH	0.0	WATER	0.1	FIRE	0.1
WOOD	0.8	THUNDER	0.1	DARKNESS	0.1

SKILLS: Mumyn Lei

DATA DRAIN ITEMS
Wrist Band, Leather Armor

SWORDMANOID — Species: Warrior (M)

LEVEL	2	SIZE	S	DATA DRAIN MONSTER	Rajin

HP/SP/PP	60/25/32	MIND/BODY RESISTANCE	1.6/3.4

PHYSICAL/MAGICAL ATK	3.7/0.7
PHYSICAL/MAGICAL DEF	5.4/2.9
PHYSICAL/MAGICAL ACC	4.0/1.6
PHYSICAL/MAGICAL EVD	0.7/0.3

EARTH	0.2	WATER	0.2	FIRE	0.2
WOOD	0.2	THUNDER	1.5	DARKNESS	0.0

SKILLS: N/A

DATA DRAIN ITEMS
Phantom Blades, Head Gear

DEADLY MOTH
Species: Bird

LEVEL	2	SIZE M	DATA DRAIN MONSTER Wiggly

HP/SP/PP 130/35/80	MIND/BODY RESISTANCE 1.6/3.0

PHYSICAL/MAGICAL ATK	3.7/2.1
PHYSICAL/MAGICAL DEF	5.4/2.9
PHYSICAL/MAGICAL ACC	4.0/3.6
PHYSICAL/MAGICAL EVD	34/0.7

EARTH	0.2	WATER	0.2	FIRE	0.2
WOOD	0.2	THUNDER	0.2	DARKNESS	0.2

SKILLS N/A

DATA DRAIN ITEMS
Earth Sword, Safety Shoes

SNIP SNAP
Species: Crustacean

LEVEL	3	SIZE M	DATA DRAIN MONSTER Monkey Crab

HP/SP/PP 170/65/110	MIND/BODY RESISTANCE 1.9/4.0

PHYSICAL/MAGICAL ATK	4.3/0.8
PHYSICAL/MAGICAL DEF	21/4.1
PHYSICAL/MAGICAL ACC	4.4/1.9
PHYSICAL/MAGICAL EVD	1.0/0.4

EARTH	0.3	WATER	0.3	FIRE	0.3
WOOD	0.3	THUNDER	0.3	DARKNESS	0.3

SKILLS N/A

DATA DRAIN ITEMS
Head Gear, Used Greaves

MAGICAL GOBLIN
Species: Goblin

LEVEL	3	SIZE S	DATA DRAIN MONSTER Gremlin

HP/SP/PP 70/35/28	MIND/BODY RESISTANCE 1.9/4.0

PHYSICAL/MAGICAL ATK	0.8/1.1
PHYSICAL/MAGICAL DEF	1.9/19.5
PHYSICAL/MAGICAL ACC	1.9/4.4
PHYSICAL/MAGICAL EVD	1.0/1.0

EARTH	0.3	WATER	0.0	FIRE	1.7
WOOD	0.3	THUNDER	0.3	DARKNESS	0.3

SKILLS Duk Lei, Ap Torma

DATA DRAIN ITEMS
Steel Blades, Leather Gloves

CHICKEN HAND
Species: Bird

LEVEL	4	SIZE S	DATA DRAIN MONSTER Chicky

HP/SP/PP 80/45/44	MIND/BODY RESISTANCE 2.2/5.0

PHYSICAL/MAGICAL ATK	4.9/0.9
PHYSICAL/MAGICAL DEF	8.8/5.3
PHYSICAL/MAGICAL ACC	6.0/2.2
PHYSICAL/MAGICAL EVD	38/0.5

EARTH	0.0	WATER	0.4	FIRE	0.4
WOOD	2.2	THUNDER	0.4	DARKNESS	0.4

SKILLS N/A

DATA DRAIN ITEMS
Battle Axe, Leather Gloves

SKY FISH
Species: Fish

LEVEL	4	SIZE S	DATA DRAIN MONSTER Fry

HP/SP/PP 90/45/44	MIND/BODY RESISTANCE 2.2/5.0

PHYSICAL/MAGICAL ATK	4.9/0.9
PHYSICAL/MAGICAL DEF	8.8/5.3
PHYSICAL/MAGICAL ACC	6.0/2.2
PHYSICAL/MAGICAL EVD	1.3/0.5

EARTH	0.4	WATER	2.2	FIRE	0.0
WOOD	0.4	THUNDER	0.4	DARKNESS	0.4

SKILLS Duk Lei

DATA DRAIN ITEMS
Mizuchi, Nomad's Hood

HEADHUNTER
Species: Undead

LEVEL	5	SIZE M	DATA DRAIN MONSTER Fophead

HP/SP/PP 250/80/170	MIND/BODY RESISTANCE 2.5/6.0

PHYSICAL/MAGICAL ATK	5.5/5.0
PHYSICAL/MAGICAL DEF	10.5/7.0
PHYSICAL/MAGICAL ACC	7.0/6.0
PHYSICAL/MAGICAL EVD	1.6/1.6

EARTH	0.5	WATER	0.5	FIRE	0.5
WOOD	0.5	THUNDER	0.0	DARKNESS	2.7

SKILLS N/A

DATA DRAIN ITEMS
Fire Spear, Ceramic Anklet

CADET VALKYRIE
Species: Warrior (F)

LEVEL	5	SIZE S	DATA DRAIN MONSTER Jiggle

HP/SP/PP 90/105/50	MIND/BODY RESISTANCE 2.5/6.0

PHYSICAL/MAGICAL ATK	5.5/1.0
PHYSICAL/MAGICAL DEF	10.5/6.5
PHYSICAL/MAGICAL ACC	7.0/2.5
PHYSICAL/MAGICAL EVD	1.6/0.6

EARTH	0.0	WATER	0.5	FIRE	0.5
WOOD	2.7	THUNDER	0.5	DARKNESS	0.5

SKILLS N/A

DATA DRAIN ITEMS
Gakaku, Plate Armor

HELL DOBERMAN
Species: Hound

LEVEL	6	SIZE M	DATA DRAIN MONSTER Pup

HP/SP/PP 290/125/200	MIND/BODY RESISTANCE 2.8/7.0

PHYSICAL/MAGICAL ATK	6.1/3.5
PHYSICAL/MAGICAL DEF	12.2/7.7
PHYSICAL/MAGICAL ACC	8.0/2.8
PHYSICAL/MAGICAL EVD	1.9/0.7

EARTH	0.6	WATER	0.0	FIRE	6.2
WOOD	0.6	THUNDER	0.6	DARKNESS	0.6

SKILLS Vak Kruz

DATA DRAIN ITEMS
Fire Spear, Hunter's Hood

BESTIARY

SWORD OF CHAOS
Species: Knife

LEVEL	6	SIZE	S	DATA DRAIN MONSTER	Gunyarin

HP/SP/PP	110/65/56	MIND/BODY RESISTANCE	19/19

PHYSICAL/MAGICAL ATK	6.1/1.1
PHYSICAL/MAGICAL DEF	12.2/7.7
PHYSICAL/MAGICAL ACC	8.0/2.8
PHYSICAL/MAGICAL EVD	1.9/0.7

EARTH	0.6	WATER	0.6	FIRE	0.6
WOOD	0.6	THUNDER	0.6	DARKNESS	0.6

SKILLS: Spin Slash (x3)

DATA DRAIN ITEMS: Fire Spear, Gakaku

MUSHROOM KING
Species: Plant

LEVEL	6	SIZE	M	DATA DRAIN MONSTER	Sunnyflower

HP/SP/PP	290/125/200	MIND/BODY RESISTANCE	2.8/7.0

PHYSICAL/MAGICAL ATK	6.1/3.5
PHYSICAL/MAGICAL DEF	12.2/7.7
PHYSICAL/MAGICAL ACC	8.0/2.8
PHYSICAL/MAGICAL EVD	1.9/0.7

EARTH	0.0	WATER	0.6	FIRE	0.6
WOOD	3.8	THUNDER	0.6	DARKNESS	0.6

SKILLS: Ap Torv

DATA DRAIN ITEMS: Fossil Bracer, Wyrm Hide

ECTOPLASM
Species: Wraith

LEVEL	6	SIZE	S	DATA DRAIN MONSTER	Boo

HP/SP/PP	218/65/80	MIND/BODY RESISTANCE	2.8/7.0

PHYSICAL/MAGICAL ATK	6.1/2.2
PHYSICAL/MAGICAL DEF	24/8.2
PHYSICAL/MAGICAL ACC	8.0/6.8
PHYSICAL/MAGICAL EVD	99/27.2

EARTH	0.6	WATER	0.6	FIRE	0.6
WOOD	0.6	THUNDER	0.0	DARKNESS	3.2

SKILLS: Ani Don

DATA DRAIN ITEMS: Fire Wand, Hiking Gear

MUMMY RIPPER
Species: Warrior (F)

LEVEL	7	SIZE	S	DATA DRAIN MONSTER	Porolin

HP/SP/PP	110/75/62	MIND/BODY RESISTANCE	3.1/8.0

PHYSICAL/MAGICAL ATK	6.7/1.2
PHYSICAL/MAGICAL DEF	13.9/8.9
PHYSICAL/MAGICAL ACC	9.0/3.1
PHYSICAL/MAGICAL EVD	2.2/0.8

EARTH	0.0	WATER	0.7	FIRE	0.7
WOOD	3.7	THUNDER	0.7	DARKNESS	0.7

SKILLS: Dek Corv

DATA DRAIN ITEMS: Strange Blade, Grand Armor

HOBGOBLIN
Species: Goblin

LEVEL	7	SIZE	S	DATA DRAIN MONSTER	Gremlin

HP/SP/PP	110/75/52	MIND/BODY RESISTANCE	3.1/8.0

PHYSICAL/MAGICAL ATK	6.7/1.2
PHYSICAL/MAGICAL DEF	13.9/8.9
PHYSICAL/MAGICAL ACC	9.0/3.1
PHYSICAL/MAGICAL EVD	2.2/0.8

EARTH	3.7	WATER	0.7	FIRE	0.7
WOOD	0.0	THUNDER	0.7	DARKNESS	0.7

SKILLS: N/A

DATA DRAIN ITEMS: Lath Blades, Miner's Gloves

FIEND MENHIR
Species: Statue

LEVEL	7	SIZE	M	DATA DRAIN MONSTER	Gruntsquirm

HP/SP/PP	330/145/230	MIND/BODY RESISTANCE	100/100

PHYSICAL/MAGICAL ATK	6.7/2.4
PHYSICAL/MAGICAL DEF	13.9/8.9
PHYSICAL/MAGICAL ACC	9.0/7.6
PHYSICAL/MAGICAL EVD	2.2/44

EARTH	0.0	WATER	0.7	FIRE	0.7
WOOD	0.7	THUNDER	3.7	DARKNESS	0.7

SKILLS: Rip Maen

DATA DRAIN ITEMS: Wind Axe, Hands of Earth

SNAKOID
Species: Lizard

LEVEL	7	SIZE	S	DATA DRAIN MONSTER	Dragon Puppy

HP/SP/PP	120/75/62	MIND/BODY RESISTANCE	8.0/8.0

PHYSICAL/MAGICAL ATK	6.7/2.4
PHYSICAL/MAGICAL DEF	13.9/8.9
PHYSICAL/MAGICAL ACC	9.0/7.6
PHYSICAL/MAGICAL EVD	2.2/2.2

EARTH	0.7	WATER	0.0	FIRE	7.2
WOOD	0.7	THUNDER	0.7	DARKNESS	0.7

SKILLS: Wild Shot (x11), Ap Corv

DATA DRAIN ITEMS: Stun Sword, Wyrm Hide

BEE ARMY
Species: Insect

LEVEL	7	SIZE	M	DATA DRAIN MONSTER	Nyororon

HP/SP/PP	330/110/230	MIND/BODY RESISTANCE	3.1/8.0

PHYSICAL/MAGICAL ATK	6.7/3.6
PHYSICAL/MAGICAL DEF	13.9/8.9
PHYSICAL/MAGICAL ACC	9.0/7.6
PHYSICAL/MAGICAL EVD	44/2.2

EARTH	0.7	WATER	0.7	FIRE	0.7
WOOD	0.7	THUNDER	0.7	DARKNESS	0.7

SKILLS: Duk Lei

DATA DRAIN ITEMS: Green Sword, Mountain Boots

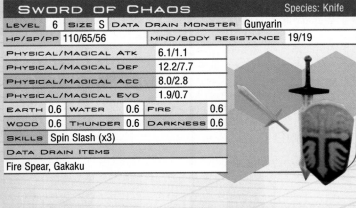

DUST CURSE
Species: Knife

LEVEL	8	SIZE	S	DATA DRAIN MONSTER	Gunyarin

HP/SP/PP	130/85/68	MIND/BODY RESISTANCE	25/25

PHYSICAL/MAGICAL ATK	7.3/1.3
PHYSICAL/MAGICAL DEF	15.6/10.1
PHYSICAL/MAGICAL ACC	10/3.4
PHYSICAL/MAGICAL EVD	2.5/0.9

EARTH	0.8	WATER	0.8	FIRE	0.8
WOOD	0.8	THUNDER	0.8	DARKNESS	0.8

SKILLS	Spin Slash (x3)

DATA DRAIN ITEMS
Wooden Spear, Strange Blade

MIMIC
Species: Mimic

LEVEL	8	SIZE	S	DATA DRAIN MONSTER	Funny Money

HP/SP/PP	370/165/260	MIND/BODY RESISTANCE	100/100

PHYSICAL/MAGICAL ATK	6.5/1.3
PHYSICAL/MAGICAL DEF	31/13
PHYSICAL/MAGICAL ACC	8.4/3.4
PHYSICAL/MAGICAL EVD	2.5/46

EARTH	0.8	WATER	0.8	FIRE	0.8
WOOD	0.8	THUNDER	0.8	DARKNESS	0.8

SKILLS	Ranki Lei

DATA DRAIN ITEMS
Hands of Earth, Fossil Bracer

SCORPION TANK
Species: Crustacean

LEVEL	9	SIZE	L	DATA DRAIN MONSTER	Monkey Crab

HP/SP/PP	770/275/560	MIND/BODY RESISTANCE	3.7/10

PHYSICAL/MAGICAL ATK	7.9/1.4
PHYSICAL/MAGICAL DEF	33/11.3
PHYSICAL/MAGICAL ACC	9.2/3.7
PHYSICAL/MAGICAL EVD	2.8/1.0

EARTH	0.9	WATER	0.9	FIRE	0.9
WOOD	0.9	THUNDER	0.9	DARKNESS	0.9

SKILLS	N/A

DATA DRAIN ITEMS
Mountain Guard, Mountain Helm

SHIELD MAN
Species: Demon

LEVEL	9	SIZE	S	DATA DRAIN MONSTER	Bat

HP/SP/PP	130/95/74	MIND/BODY RESISTANCE	19/10

PHYSICAL/MAGICAL ATK	7.9/2.8
PHYSICAL/MAGICAL DEF	17.3/25.8
PHYSICAL/MAGICAL ACC	11/9.2
PHYSICAL/MAGICAL EVD	2.8/48

EARTH	0.9	WATER	0.9	FIRE	0.9
WOOD	0.9	THUNDER	0.0	DARKNESS	5.6

SKILLS	Dek Torv

DATA DRAIN ITEMS
Fuse Blades, Cougar Bandana

ROCK HEAD
Species: Earth Elemental

LEVEL	9	SIZE	M	DATA DRAIN MONSTER	Moai

HP/SP/PP	410/185/290	MIND/BODY RESISTANCE	3.7/19

PHYSICAL/MAGICAL ATK	7.9/1.4
PHYSICAL/MAGICAL DEF	33/11.3
PHYSICAL/MAGICAL ACC	9.2/3.7
PHYSICAL/MAGICAL EVD	2.8/1.0

EARTH	4.7	WATER	0.9	FIRE	0.9
WOOD	0.0	THUNDER	0.9	DARKNESS	0.9

SKILLS	Rig Saem

DATA DRAIN ITEMS
Thunder Axe, Mountain Guard

RED WYRM
Species: Lizard

LEVEL	10	SIZE	L	DATA DRAIN MONSTER	Dragon Puppy

HP/SP/PP	850/105/620	MIND/BODY RESISTANCE	11/11

PHYSICAL/MAGICAL ATK	8.5/3.0
PHYSICAL/MAGICAL DEF	19/12.5
PHYSICAL/MAGICAL ACC	12/10
PHYSICAL/MAGICAL EVD	3.1/3.1

EARTH	1.0	WATER	0.0	FIRE	102
WOOD	1.0	THUNDER	1.0	DARKNESS	1.0

SKILLS	Breath, Vak Don

DATA DRAIN ITEMS
Defense Sword, Firedrake Mail

CYCLO SHARK
Species: Fish

LEVEL	11	SIZE	L	DATA DRAIN MONSTER	Fry

HP/SP/PP	930/225/680	MIND/BODY RESISTANCE	4.3/12

PHYSICAL/MAGICAL ATK	13.5/1.6
PHYSICAL/MAGICAL DEF	20.7/13.7
PHYSICAL/MAGICAL ACC	13/4.3
PHYSICAL/MAGICAL EVD	3.4/1.2

EARTH	1.1	WATER	5.7	FIRE	0.0
WOOD	1.1	THUNDER	1.1	DARKNESS	1.1

SKILLS	Rue Kruz

DATA DRAIN ITEMS
Unicorn Blade, Ice Hunter Hat

HUNGRY GRASS
Species: Plant

LEVEL	11	SIZE	S	DATA DRAIN MONSTER	Sunnyflower

HP/SP/PP	160/115/86	MIND/BODY RESISTANCE	4.3/12

PHYSICAL/MAGICAL ATK	9.1/6.0
PHYSICAL/MAGICAL DEF	20.7/13.7
PHYSICAL/MAGICAL ACC	13/4.3
PHYSICAL/MAGICAL EVD	3.4/1.2

EARTH	0.0	WATER	1.1	FIRE	1.1
WOOD	6.8	THUNDER	1.1	DARKNESS	1.1

SKILLS	Mumyn Lei

DATA DRAIN ITEMS
Frost Bracer, Wyrm Scale

GUARDIAN

Species: Golem

LEVEL	12	SIZE	M	DATA DRAIN MONSTER	Scarecrooner

HP/SP/PP	530/245/380	MIND/BODY RESISTANCE	100/100

PHYSICAL/MAGICAL ATK	9.7/1.7
PHYSICAL/MAGICAL DEF	39/14.9
PHYSICAL/MAGICAL ACC	14/4.6
PHYSICAL/MAGICAL EVD	3.7/1.3

EARTH	7.4	WATER	1.2	FIRE	1.2
WOOD	0.0	THUNDER	1.2	DARKNESS	1.2

SKILLS N/A

DATA DRAIN ITEMS

Razor Axe, Frost Armor

CRAB TURTLE

Species: Crustacean

LEVEL	12	SIZE	M	DATA DRAIN MONSTER	Monkey Crab

HP/SP/PP	530/245/380	MIND/BODY RESISTANCE	4.6/13

PHYSICAL/MAGICAL ATK	9.7/1.7
PHYSICAL/MAGICAL DEF	39/14.9
PHYSICAL/MAGICAL ACC	11.6/4.6
PHYSICAL/MAGICAL EVD	3.7/1.3

EARTH	1.2	WATER	1.2	FIRE	1.2
WOOD	1.2	THUNDER	1.2	DARKNESS	1.2

SKILLS N/A

DATA DRAIN ITEMS

Aqua Guard, Ice Helm

FLAME HEADS

Species: Hound

LEVEL	12	SIZE	L	DATA DRAIN MONSTER	Pup

HP/SP/PP	1010/365/740	MIND/BODY RESISTANCE	4.6/13

PHYSICAL/MAGICAL ATK	9.7/6.5
PHYSICAL/MAGICAL DEF	22.4/14.9
PHYSICAL/MAGICAL ACC	14/4.6
PHYSICAL/MAGICAL EVD	3.7/1.3

EARTH	1.2	WATER	0.0	FIRE	12.2
WOOD	1.2	THUNDER	1.2	DARKNESS	1.2

SKILLS Breath (x4), Vak Rom

DATA DRAIN ITEMS

Gold Spear, Ice Hunter Hat

STONE TURTLE

Species: Earth Elemental

LEVEL	13	SIZE	L	DATA DRAIN MONSTER	Moai

HP/SP/PP	1090/1090/800	MIND/BODY RESISTANCE	4.9/27

PHYSICAL/MAGICAL ATK	10.3/1.8
PHYSICAL/MAGICAL DEF	41/16.1
PHYSICAL/MAGICAL ACC	12.4/4.9
PHYSICAL/MAGICAL EVD	4.0/1.4

EARTH	6.7	WATER	1.3	FIRE	1.3
WOOD	0.0	THUNDER	1.3	DARKNESS	1.3

SKILLS Rig Saem

DATA DRAIN ITEMS

Razor Axe, Aqua Guard

THOUSAND TREES

Species: Plant

LEVEL	13	SIZE	L	DATA DRAIN MONSTER	Sunnyflower

HP/SP/PP	1090/395/800	MIND/BODY RESISTANCE	4.9/14

PHYSICAL/MAGICAL ATK	10.3/7.0
PHYSICAL/MAGICAL DEF	24.1/16.1
PHYSICAL/MAGICAL ACC	15/4.9
PHYSICAL/MAGICAL EVD	4.0/1.4

EARTH	0.0	WATER	1.3	FIRE	1.3
WOOD	8.0	THUNDER	1.3	DARKNESS	1.3

SKILLS Juk Rom, Juk Zot

DATA DRAIN ITEMS

Frost Bracer, Wyrm Scale

HEAVY METAL

Species: Warrior (M)

LEVEL	14	SIZE	S	DATA DRAIN MONSTER	Rajin

HP/SP/PP	180/145/104	MIND/BODY RESISTANCE	5.2/17.8

PHYSICAL/MAGICAL ATK	10.9/1.9
PHYSICAL/MAGICAL DEF	25.8/17.3
PHYSICAL/MAGICAL ACC	16/5.2
PHYSICAL/MAGICAL EVD	4.3/1.5

EARTH	1.4	WATER	1.4	FIRE	1.4
WOOD	1.4	THUNDER	7.5	DARKNESS	0.0

SKILLS N/A

DATA DRAIN ITEMS

Ronin Blades, Ice Helm

WATER WITCH

Species: Magic-User (F)

LEVEL	14	SIZE	S	DATA DRAIN MONSTER	Mew-Burn

HP/SP/PP	180/145/52	MIND/BODY RESISTANCE	5.2/15

PHYSICAL/MAGICAL ATK	1.9/8.6
PHYSICAL/MAGICAL DEF	5.2/43.5
PHYSICAL/MAGICAL ACC	5.2/17.2
PHYSICAL/MAGICAL EVD	4.3/68

EARTH	1.4	WATER	7.2	FIRE	0.0
WOOD	1.4	THUNDER	1.4	DARKNESS	1.4

SKILLS Rue Kruz, Rue Zot

DATA DRAIN ITEMS

Basho Wand, Winter Coat

GOBLIN NIGHT

Species: Goblin

LEVEL	15	SIZE	S	DATA DRAIN MONSTER	Gremlin

HP/SP/PP	190/155/100	MIND/BODY RESISTANCE	5.5/16

PHYSICAL/MAGICAL ATK	11.5/1.2
PHYSICAL/MAGICAL DEF	27.5/18.5
PHYSICAL/MAGICAL ACC	17/5.5
PHYSICAL/MAGICAL EVD	4.6/1.6

EARTH	7.7	WATER	1.5	FIRE	1.5
WOOD	0.0	THUNDER	1.5	DARKNESS	1.5

SKILLS N/A

DATA DRAIN ITEMS

Spell Blades, Fishing Gloves

SLED DOG
Species: Hound

LEVEL	15	SIZE M DATA DRAIN MONSTER Pup

HP/SP/PP 650/305/470	MIND/BODY RESISTANCE 5.5/16

PHYSICAL/MAGICAL ATK	11.5/8.0
PHYSICAL/MAGICAL DEF	27.5/18.5
PHYSICAL/MAGICAL ACC	17/5.5
PHYSICAL/MAGICAL EVD	4.6/1.6

EARTH	1.5	WATER	0.0	FIRE	15.2
WOOD	1.5	THUNDER	1.5	DARKNESS	1.5

SKILLS Vak Don

DATA DRAIN ITEMS

Spear of Spell, Ice Hunter Hat

LAMIA FIGHTER
Species: Snake

LEVEL	15	SIZE S DATA DRAIN MONSTER Snake-Charmer

HP/SP/PP 200/155/110	MIND/BODY RESISTANCE 5.5/16

PHYSICAL/MAGICAL ATK	11.5/7.0
PHYSICAL/MAGICAL DEF	27.5/33
PHYSICAL/MAGICAL ACC	17/14
PHYSICAL/MAGICAL EVD	4.6/60

EARTH	7.7	WATER	1.5	FIRE	1.5
WOOD	0.0	THUNDER	1.5	DARKNESS	1.5

SKILLS Bite (x5), Mumyn Lei

DATA DRAIN ITEMS

Oak Anklet, Ranger's Boots

NOMADIC BONES
Species: Undead

LEVEL	15	SIZE S DATA DRAIN MONSTER Fophead

HP/SP/PP 200/155/110	MIND/BODY RESISTANCE 5.5/16

PHYSICAL/MAGICAL ATK	11.5/10
PHYSICAL/MAGICAL DEF	27.5/19
PHYSICAL/MAGICAL ACC	17/14
PHYSICAL/MAGICAL EVD	4.6/4.6

EARTH	1.5	WATER	1.5	FIRE	1.5
WOOD	1.5	THUNDER	0.0	DARKNESS	7.7

SKILLS N/A

DATA DRAIN ITEMS

Spear of Spell, Frost Anklet

SHINING EYES
Species: Wraith

LEVEL	15	SIZE M DATA DRAIN MONSTER Odoro

HP/SP/PP 650/305/470	MIND/BODY RESISTANCE 5.5/16

PHYSICAL/MAGICAL ATK	11.5/4.0
PHYSICAL/MAGICAL DEF	37.5/19
PHYSICAL/MAGICAL ACC	17/14
PHYSICAL/MAGICAL EVD	99/38

EARTH	1.5	WATER	1.5	FIRE	1.5
WOOD	1.5	THUNDER	0.0	DARKNESS	7.7

SKILLS Ani Don

DATA DRAIN ITEMS

Diabolic Wand, Winter Coat

OCHIMUSHA
Species: Warrior (M)

LEVEL	16	SIZE S DATA DRAIN MONSTER Rajin

HP/SP/PP 200/165/116	MIND/BODY RESISTANCE 5.8/20.2

PHYSICAL/MAGICAL ATK	12.1/2.1
PHYSICAL/MAGICAL DEF	29.2/19.7
PHYSICAL/MAGICAL ACC	18/5.8
PHYSICAL/MAGICAL EVD	4.9/1.7

EARTH	1.6	WATER	1.6	FIRE	1.6
WOOD	1.6	THUNDER	8.5	DARKNESS	0.0

SKILLS Ap Corv

DATA DRAIN ITEMS

Spell Blades, Fire Helm

SQUILLA DEMON
Species: Crustacean

LEVEL	16	SIZE M DATA DRAIN MONSTER Monkey Crab

HP/SP/PP 690/325/500	MIND/BODY RESISTANCE 5.8/17

PHYSICAL/MAGICAL ATK	12.1/2.1
PHYSICAL/MAGICAL DEF	47/19.7
PHYSICAL/MAGICAL ACC	14.8/5.8
PHYSICAL/MAGICAL EVD	4.9/1.7

EARTH	1.6	WATER	1.6	FIRE	1.6
WOOD	1.6	THUNDER	1.6	DARKNESS	1.6

SKILLS Ap Corv

DATA DRAIN ITEMS

Ice Helm, Aqua Guard

GOBLIN WIZ
Species: Goblin

LEVEL	16	SIZE S DATA DRAIN MONSTER Gremlin

HP/SP/PP 200/165/106	MIND/BODY RESISTANCE 5.8/17

PHYSICAL/MAGICAL ATK	2.1/3.7
PHYSICAL/MAGICAL DEF	5.8/39
PHYSICAL/MAGICAL ACC	5.8/14.8
PHYSICAL/MAGICAL EVD	4.9/4.9

EARTH	1.6	WATER	0.0	FIRE	8.2
WOOD	1.6	THUNDER	1.6	DARKNESS	1.6

SKILLS BiVak Rom, Dek Vorma

DATA DRAIN ITEMS

Spell Blades, Smith's Gloves

KILLER SNAKER
Species: Snake

LEVEL	16	SIZE L DATA DRAIN MONSTER Snake-Charmer

HP/SP/PP 1330/485/970	MIND/BODY RESISTANCE 5.8/17

PHYSICAL/MAGICAL ATK	12.1/7.4
PHYSICAL/MAGICAL DEF	29.2/34.2
PHYSICAL/MAGICAL ACC	18/14.8
PHYSICAL/MAGICAL EVD	4.9/62

EARTH	8.2	WATER	1.6	FIRE	1.6
WOOD	0.0	THUNDER	1.6	DARKNESS	1.6

SKILLS Gan Rom

DATA DRAIN ITEMS

Iron Anklet, Fire Lizard

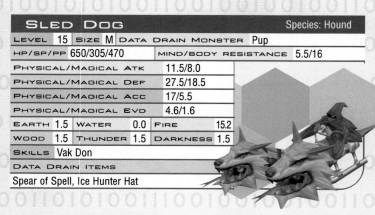

METAL EMPEROR
Species: Golem

LEVEL	17	SIZE	M	DATA DRAIN MONSTER	Kakasinger

HP/SP/PP	730/345/530	MIND/BODY RESISTANCE	100/100

PHYSICAL/MAGICAL ATK	12.7/2.2
PHYSICAL/MAGICAL DEF	49/20.9
PHYSICAL/MAGICAL ACC	19/6.1
PHYSICAL/MAGICAL EVD	5.2/1.8

EARTH	10.4	WATER	1.7	FIRE	1.7
WOOD	0.0	THUNDER	1.7	DARKNESS	1.7

SKILLS: Triple Crush

DATA DRAIN ITEMS: Earth Axe, Blaze Armor

ARROW FISH
Species: Fish

LEVEL	17	SIZE	S	DATA DRAIN MONSTER	Fry

HP/SP/PP	220/175/122	MIND/BODY RESISTANCE	6.1/20

PHYSICAL/MAGICAL ATK	12.7/2.2
PHYSICAL/MAGICAL DEF	30.9/20.9
PHYSICAL/MAGICAL ACC	19/6.1
PHYSICAL/MAGICAL EVD	5.2/1.8

EARTH	1.7	WATER	8.7	FIRE	0.0
WOOD	1.7	THUNDER	1.7	DARKNESS	1.7

SKILLS: Duk Lei

DATA DRAIN ITEMS: Earth Crest Blade – Fugaku, Fire Dance Hat

MENHIR
Species: Statue

LEVEL	17	SIZE	M	DATA DRAIN MONSTER	Hebinyoro

HP/SP/PP	730/345/530	MIND/BODY RESISTANCE	100/100

PHYSICAL/MAGICAL ATK	12.7/4.4
PHYSICAL/MAGICAL DEF	30.9/20.9
PHYSICAL/MAGICAL ACC	19/15.6
PHYSICAL/MAGICAL EVD	5.2/64

EARTH	0.0	WATER	1.7	FIRE	1.7
WOOD	1.7	THUNDER	8.7	DARKNESS	1.7

SKILLS: Rip Maen

DATA DRAIN ITEMS: Earth Axe, Hands of Fire

SCARLET KING
Species: Plant

LEVEL	17	SIZE	M	DATA DRAIN MONSTER	Sunnyflower

HP/SP/PP	730/345/530	MIND/BODY RESISTANCE	6.1/18

PHYSICAL/MAGICAL ATK	12.7/9.0
PHYSICAL/MAGICAL DEF	30.9/20.9
PHYSICAL/MAGICAL ACC	19/6.1
PHYSICAL/MAGICAL EVD	5.2/1.8

EARTH	0.0	WATER	1.7	FIRE	1.7
WOOD	10.4	THUNDER	1.7	DARKNESS	1.7

SKILLS: Ap Corv

DATA DRAIN ITEMS: Fire Bracer, Firedrake Mail

PHANTOM WING
Species: Insect

LEVEL	18	SIZE	M	DATA DRAIN MONSTER	Nyororon

HP/SP/PP	770/275/560	MIND/BODY RESISTANCE	6.4/19

PHYSICAL/MAGICAL ATK	13.3/6.9
PHYSICAL/MAGICAL DEF	32.6/22.1
PHYSICAL/MAGICAL ACC	20/16.4
PHYSICAL/MAGICAL EVD	66/5.5

EARTH	1.8	WATER	1.8	FIRE	1.8
WOOD	1.8	THUNDER	1.8	DARKNESS	1.8

SKILLS: Duk Lei

DATA DRAIN ITEMS: Shanato, Fire Lizard

NOISY WISP
Species: Wraith

LEVEL	18	SIZE	S	DATA DRAIN MONSTER	Odoro

HP/SP/PP	554/185/200	MIND/BODY RESISTANCE	6.4/19

PHYSICAL/MAGICAL ATK	13.3/4.6
PHYSICAL/MAGICAL DEF	42/22.6
PHYSICAL/MAGICAL ACC	20/16.4
PHYSICAL/MAGICAL EVD	99/41.6

EARTH	1.8	WATER	1.8	FIRE	1.8
WOOD	1.8	THUNDER	0.0	DARKNESS	9.2

SKILLS: Ani Don

DATA DRAIN ITEMS: Earth Rod, Fireman's Coat

GENERAL ARMOR
Species: Warrior (M)

LEVEL	19	SIZE	M	DATA DRAIN MONSTER	Rajin

HP/SP/PP	810/385/590	MIND/BODY RESISTANCE	6.7/23.8

PHYSICAL/MAGICAL ATK	13.9/2.4
PHYSICAL/MAGICAL DEF	34.3/23.3
PHYSICAL/MAGICAL ACC	21/6.7
PHYSICAL/MAGICAL EVD	5.8/2.0

EARTH	1.9	WATER	1.9	FIRE	1.9
WOOD	1.9	THUNDER	10	DARKNESS	0.0

SKILLS: Iron Ball (x3)

DATA DRAIN ITEMS: Sotetsu, Fire Helm

DARK WITCH
Species: Magic-User (F)

LEVEL	19	SIZE	S	DATA DRAIN MONSTER	Moenyan

HP/SP/PP	230/195/67	MIND/BODY RESISTANCE	6.7/20

PHYSICAL/MAGICAL ATK	2.4/8.6
PHYSICAL/MAGICAL DEF	6.7/43.5
PHYSICAL/MAGICAL ACC	6.7/17.2
PHYSICAL/MAGICAL EVD	5.8/68

EARTH	1.9	WATER	1.9	FIRE	1.9
WOOD	1.9	THUNDER	0.0	DARKNESS	9.7

SKILLS: MeAni Kruz, MeAni Zot

DATA DRAIN ITEMS: Rod of the Sea, Fireman's Coat

WOOD HARPY

Species: Bird

Level	19	Size	S	Data Drain Monster	Piyoko-San

HP/SP/PP	230/195/134	Mind/Body Resistance	6.7/20

Physical/Magical Atk	13.9/2.4
Physical/Magical Def	34.3/23.3
Physical/Magical Acc	21/6.7
Physical/Magical Evd	68/2.0

Earth	0.0	Water	1.9	Fire	1.9
Wood	9.7	Thunder	1.9	Darkness	1.9

Skills	N/A

Data Drain Items

Water God Axe, Smith's Gloves

FIRE WATCH

Species: Magic-User (F)

Level	20	Size	S	Data Drain Monster	Moenyan

HP/SP/PP	240/205/70	Mind/Body Resistance	7.0/21

Physical/Magical Atk	2.5/9.0
Physical/Magical Def	7.0/45
Physical/Magical Acc	7.0/18
Physical/Magical Evd	6.1/58

Earth	2.0	Water	0.0	Fire	10.2
Wood	2.0	Thunder	2.0	Darkness	2.0

Skills	GiVak Don, GiVak Kruz

Data Drain Items

Inferno Wand, Lincoln Green

LAMBADA KNIFE

Species: Knife

Level	20	Size	S	Data Drain Monster	Gunyarin

HP/SP/PP	250/405/140	Mind/Body Resistance	61/61

Physical/Magical Atk	14.5/2.5
Physical/Magical Def	36/24.5
Physical/Magical Acc	22/7.0
Physical/Magical Evd	6.1/2.1

Earth	2.0	Water	2.0	Fire	2.0
Wood	2.0	Thunder	2.0	Darkness	2.0

Skills	N/A

Data Drain Items

Lavaman Spear, Komura

GLADIATOR

Species: Warrior (M)

Level	21	Size	S	Data Drain Monster	Rajin

HP/SP/PP	250/215/146	Mind/Body Resistance	5.8/20.2

Physical/Magical Atk	15.1/2.6
Physical/Magical Def	37.7/25.7
Physical/Magical Acc	23/7.3
Physical/Magical Evd	6.4/2.2

Earth	2.1	Water	2.1	Fire	2.1
Wood	2.1	Thunder	11	Darkness	0.0

Skills	N/A

Data Drain Items

Enou, Forester Helm

FRESH VALKYRIE

Species: Warrior (F)

Level	21	Size	S	Data Drain Monster	Porolin

HP/SP/PP	250/215/146	Mind/Body Resistance	7.3/22

Physical/Magical Atk	15.1/2.6
Physical/Magical Def	37.7/25.7
Physical/Magical Acc	23/7.3
Physical/Magical Evd	6.4/2.2

Earth	0.0	Water	2.1	Fire	2.1
Wood	10.7	Thunder	2.1	Darkness	2.1

Skills	La Repth

Data Drain Items

Komura, Spirit Armor

HELL BOX

Species: Mimic

Level	22	Size	S	Data Drain Monster	Funny Money

HP/SP/PP	930/445/680	Mind/Body Resistance	100/100

Physical/Magical Atk	13.5/2.7
Physical/Magical Def	59/34
Physical/Magical Acc	19.6/7.6
Physical/Magical Evd	6.7/74

Earth	2.2	Water	2.2	Fire	2.2
Wood	2.2	Thunder	2.2	Darkness	2.2

Skills	Ranki Lei

Data Drain Items

Hands of Wood, Air Bracer

LIVING DEAD

Species: Undead

Level	22	Size	M	Data Drain Monster	Fophead

HP/SP/PP	930/335/680	Mind/Body Resistance	7.6/23

Physical/Magical Atk	15.7/13.5
Physical/Magical Def	39.4/27.4
Physical/Magical Acc	24/19.6
Physical/Magical Evd	6.7/6.7

Earth	2.2	Water	2.2	Fire	2.2
Wood	2.2	Thunder	0.0	Darkness	11.2

Skills	Suvi Lei

Data Drain Items

Treeman Spear, Oak Anklet

GRAND MAGE

Species: Magic-User (M)

Level	23	Size	S	Data Drain Monster	Old-Timer

HP/SP/PP	270/235/125	Mind/Body Resistance	7.9/24

Physical/Magical Atk	2.8/10.2
Physical/Magical Def	7.9/49.5
Physical/Magical Acc	7.9/20.4
Physical/Magical Evd	7.0/76

Earth	2.3	Water	0.0	Fire	11.7
Wood	2.3	Thunder	2.3	Darkness	2.3

Skills	GiVak Don, Ap Vakz

Data Drain Items

Cedar Wand, Scarab Earring

LAMIA HUNTER
Species: Snake

LEVEL	23	SIZE	S	DATA DRAIN MONSTER	Snake-Charmer

HP/SP/PP	200/155/110	MIND/BODY RESISTANCE	5.5/16

PHYSICAL/MAGICAL ATK	11.5/7.0
PHYSICAL/MAGICAL DEF	27.5/33
PHYSICAL/MAGICAL ACC	17/14
PHYSICAL/MAGICAL EVD	4.6/60

EARTH	7.7	WATER	1.5	FIRE	1.5
WOOD	0.0	THUNDER	1.5	DARKNESS	1.5

SKILLS	Bite (x5)

DATA DRAIN ITEMS

Oak Anklet, Ranger's Boots

BABY WORM
Species: Insect

LEVEL	23	SIZE	L	DATA DRAIN MONSTER	Nyororon

HP/SP/PP	1890/695/1400	MIND/BODY RESISTANCE	7.9/24

PHYSICAL/MAGICAL ATK	16.3/8.4
PHYSICAL/MAGICAL DEF	41.1/28.1
PHYSICAL/MAGICAL ACC	25/20.4
PHYSICAL/MAGICAL EVD	76/7.0

EARTH	2.3	WATER	2.3	FIRE	2.3
WOOD	2.3	THUNDER	2.3	DARKNESS	2.3

SKILLS	Suvi Lei

DATA DRAIN ITEMS

Shidan, Ranger's Boots

HAMMER SHARK
Species: Fish

LEVEL	24	SIZE	L	DATA DRAIN MONSTER	Fry

HP/SP/PP	1970/485/1460	MIND/BODY RESISTANCE	8.2/25

PHYSICAL/MAGICAL ATK	26.5/2.9
PHYSICAL/MAGICAL DEF	42.8/29.3
PHYSICAL/MAGICAL ACC	26/8.2
PHYSICAL/MAGICAL EVD	7.3/2.5

EARTH	2.4	WATER	12.2	FIRE	0.0
WOOD	2.4	THUNDER	2.4	DARKNESS	2.4

SKILLS	N/A

DATA DRAIN ITEMS

Singing Blade, Peasant's Hat

IRONBALL
Species: Goblin

LEVEL	24	SIZE	L	DATA DRAIN MONSTER	Gremlin

HP/SP/PP	1970/725/1460	MIND/BODY RESISTANCE	8.2/25

PHYSICAL/MAGICAL ATK	16.9/2.9
PHYSICAL/MAGICAL DEF	42.8/29.3
PHYSICAL/MAGICAL ACC	26/8.2
PHYSICAL/MAGICAL EVD	7.3/2.5

EARTH	2.4	WATER	2.4	FIRE	2.4
WOOD	2.4	THUNDER	12.2	DARKNESS	0.0

SKILLS	Two-Hand Bash (x2)

DATA DRAIN ITEMS

Raitei, Forest Gloves

ARMOR SHOGUN
Species: Knife

LEVEL	24	SIZE	M	DATA DRAIN MONSTER	Gunyarin

HP/SP/PP	1010/485/740	MIND/BODY RESISTANCE	73/73

PHYSICAL/MAGICAL ATK	16.9/2.9
PHYSICAL/MAGICAL DEF	42.8/29.3
PHYSICAL/MAGICAL ACC	26/8.2
PHYSICAL/MAGICAL EVD	7.3/2.5

EARTH	2.4	WATER	2.4	FIRE	2.4
WOOD	2.4	THUNDER	2.4	DARKNESS	2.4

SKILLS	Two-Hand Slash (x7), Ap Vorv

DATA DRAIN ITEMS

Singing Blade, Strormer Spear

SNAPPY GRASS
Species: Plant

LEVEL	24	SIZE	S	DATA DRAIN MONSTER	Sunnyflower

HP/SP/PP	290/245/164	MIND/BODY RESISTANCE	8.2/25

PHYSICAL/MAGICAL ATK	16.9/12.5
PHYSICAL/MAGICAL DEF	42.8/29.3
PHYSICAL/MAGICAL ACC	26/8.2
PHYSICAL/MAGICAL EVD	7.3/2.5

EARTH	0.0	WATER	2.4	FIRE	2.4
WOOD	14.6	THUNDER	2.4	DARKNESS	2.4

SKILLS	Mumyn Lei

DATA DRAIN ITEMS

Oak Anklet, Holy Tree Mail

CANNIBAL
Species: Goblin

LEVEL	25	SIZE	L	DATA DRAIN MONSTER	Gremlin

HP/SP/PP	2050/755/1520	MIND/BODY RESISTANCE	8.5/26

PHYSICAL/MAGICAL ATK	17.5/3.0
PHYSICAL/MAGICAL DEF	44.5/30.5
PHYSICAL/MAGICAL ACC	27/8.5
PHYSICAL/MAGICAL EVD	7.6/2.6

EARTH	12.7	WATER	2.5	FIRE	2.5
WOOD	0.0	THUNDER	2.5	DARKNESS	2.5

SKILLS	N/A

DATA DRAIN ITEMS

Anshou, Air Bracer

LEAD SNAKOID
Species: Lizard

LEVEL	25	SIZE	S	DATA DRAIN MONSTER	Dragon Puppy

HP/SP/PP	300/255/170	MIND/BODY RESISTANCE	26/26

PHYSICAL/MAGICAL ATK	17.5/6.0
PHYSICAL/MAGICAL DEF	44.5/30.5
PHYSICAL/MAGICAL ACC	27/22
PHYSICAL/MAGICAL EVD	7.6/7.6

EARTH	2.5	WATER	0.0	FIRE	25.2
WOOD	2.5	THUNDER	2.5	DARKNESS	2.5

SKILLS	Two-Hand Slash (x7)

DATA DRAIN ITEMS

Kikujumonji, Holy Tree Mail

HALLOWEEN
Species: Wraith

LEVEL	25	SIZE	M	DATA DRAIN MONSTER	Odoro

HP/SP/PP	1050/505/770	MIND/BODY RESISTANCE	8.5/26

PHYSICAL/MAGICAL ATK	17.5/6.0
PHYSICAL/MAGICAL DEF	52.5/31
PHYSICAL/MAGICAL ACC	27/22
PHYSICAL/MAGICAL EVD	99/50

EARTH	2.5	WATER	2.5	FIRE	2.5
WOOD	2.5	THUNDER	0.0	DARKNESS	12.7

SKILLS	Spin Slash (x7), Ani Don
DATA DRAIN ITEMS	
Adian's Rod, Lincoln Green	

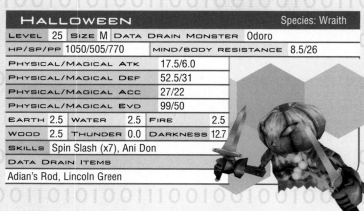

DARK RIDER
Species: Warrior (M)

LEVEL	26	SIZE	M	DATA DRAIN MONSTER	Rajin

HP/SP/PP	1090/525/800	MIND/BODY RESISTANCE	8.8/32.2

PHYSICAL/MAGICAL ATK	18.1/3.1
PHYSICAL/MAGICAL DEF	46.2/31.7
PHYSICAL/MAGICAL ACC	28/8.8
PHYSICAL/MAGICAL EVD	7.9/2.7

EARTH	2.6	WATER	2.6	FIRE	2.6
WOOD	2.6	THUNDER	0.0	DARKNESS	13.5

SKILLS	BiAni Don
DATA DRAIN ITEMS	
Anshou, Forester Helm	

METAL GOBLIN
Species: Goblin

LEVEL	26	SIZE	S	DATA DRAIN MONSTER	Gremlin

HP/SP/PP	300/265/166	MIND/BODY RESISTANCE	8.8/27

PHYSICAL/MAGICAL ATK	18.1/3.1
PHYSICAL/MAGICAL DEF	46.2/31.7
PHYSICAL/MAGICAL ACC	28/8.8
PHYSICAL/MAGICAL EVD	7.9/2.7

EARTH	13.2	WATER	2.6	FIRE	2.6
WOOD	0.0	THUNDER	2.6	DARKNESS	2.6

SKILLS	N/A
DATA DRAIN ITEMS	
Anshou, Jinsaran	

BEE ASSAULT
Species: Insect

LEVEL	26	SIZE	M	DATA DRAIN MONSTER	Nyororon

HP/SP/PP	1090/395/800	MIND/BODY RESISTANCE	8.8/27

PHYSICAL/MAGICAL ATK	18.1/9.3
PHYSICAL/MAGICAL DEF	46.2/31.7
PHYSICAL/MAGICAL ACC	28/22.8
PHYSICAL/MAGICAL EVD	82/7.9

EARTH	2.6	WATER	2.6	FIRE	2.6
WOOD	2.6	THUNDER	2.6	DARKNESS	2.6

SKILLS	Duk Lei
DATA DRAIN ITEMS	
Sharp Blade, Ranger's Boots	

MANTIS
Species: Crustacean

LEVEL	27	SIZE	M	DATA DRAIN MONSTER	Monkey Crab

HP/SP/PP	1130/545/830	MIND/BODY RESISTANCE	9.1/28

PHYSICAL/MAGICAL ATK	18.7/3.2
PHYSICAL/MAGICAL DEF	69/32.9
PHYSICAL/MAGICAL ACC	23.6/9.1
PHYSICAL/MAGICAL EVD	8.2/2.8

EARTH	2.7	WATER	2.7	FIRE	2.7
WOOD	2.7	THUNDER	2.7	DARKNESS	2.7

SKILLS	Ap Corv
DATA DRAIN ITEMS	
Giant Hill, Electric Guard	

OGRE
Species: Goblin

LEVEL	27	SIZE	L	DATA DRAIN MONSTER	Gremlin

HP/SP/PP	2210/815/1640	MIND/BODY RESISTANCE	9.1/28

PHYSICAL/MAGICAL ATK	18.7/3.2
PHYSICAL/MAGICAL DEF	47.9/32.9
PHYSICAL/MAGICAL ACC	29/9.1
PHYSICAL/MAGICAL EVD	8.2/2.8

EARTH	2.7	WATER	0.0	FIRE	13.7
WOOD	2.7	THUNDER	2.7	DARKNESS	2.7

SKILLS	N/A
DATA DRAIN ITEMS	
Masterblades, Thunder Gloves	

WOOD STOCK
Species: Plant

LEVEL	27	SIZE	L	DATA DRAIN MONSTER	Sunnyflower

HP/SP/PP	2210/815/1640	MIND/BODY RESISTANCE	9.1/28

PHYSICAL/MAGICAL ATK	18.7/14
PHYSICAL/MAGICAL DEF	47.9/32.9
PHYSICAL/MAGICAL ACC	29/9.1
PHYSICAL/MAGICAL EVD	8.2/2.8

EARTH	0.0	WATER	2.7	FIRE	2.7
WOOD	16.4	THUNDER	2.7	DARKNESS	2.7

SKILLS	RaJuk Rom
DATA DRAIN ITEMS	
Storm Bracer, Jester's Wand	

MU GUARDIAN
Species: Golem

LEVEL	28	SIZE	M	DATA DRAIN MONSTER	Kakasinger

HP/SP/PP	1170/565/860	MIND/BODY RESISTANCE	100/100

PHYSICAL/MAGICAL ATK	19.3/14.5
PHYSICAL/MAGICAL DEF	71/42.5
PHYSICAL/MAGICAL ACC	30/9.4
PHYSICAL/MAGICAL EVD	8.5/14.1

EARTH	17	WATER	2.8	FIRE	2.8
WOOD	0.0	THUNDER	2.8	DARKNESS	2.8

SKILLS	Gan Rom, GiGan Zot
DATA DRAIN ITEMS	
Bom-Ba-Ye, Master's Axe	

GOIL MENHIR

Species: Statue

LEVEL	28	SIZE	M	DATA DRAIN MONSTER	Hebinyoro

HP/SP/PP	1170/565/860	MIND/BODY RESISTANCE	100/100

PHYSICAL/MAGICAL ATK	19.3/2.4
PHYSICAL/MAGICAL DEF	49.6/8.9
PHYSICAL/MAGICAL ACC	30/7.6
PHYSICAL/MAGICAL EVD	8.5/44

EARTH	0.0	WATER	2.8	FIRE	2.8
WOOD	2.8	THUNDER	14.2	DARKNESS	2.8

SKILLS	Rip Maen

DATA DRAIN ITEMS
Master's Axe, Shikisokuzeku

CURSED BLADES

Species: Knife

LEVEL	28	SIZE	S	DATA DRAIN MONSTER	Gunyarin

HP/SP/PP	330/285/188	MIND/BODY RESISTANCE	85/85

PHYSICAL/MAGICAL ATK	19.3/3.3
PHYSICAL/MAGICAL DEF	49.6/34.1
PHYSICAL/MAGICAL ACC	30/9.4
PHYSICAL/MAGICAL EVD	8.5/2.9

EARTH	2.0	WATER	2.8	FIRE	2.8
WOOD	2.8	THUNDER	2.8	DARKNESS	2.8

SKILLS	Spin Slash (x3)

DATA DRAIN ITEMS
Sleipnir, Million $ Spear

RED SCISSORS

Species: Crustacean

LEVEL	29	SIZE	M	DATA DRAIN MONSTER	Monkey Crab

HP/SP/PP	1210/585/890	MIND/BODY RESISTANCE	9.7/30

PHYSICAL/MAGICAL ATK	18.1/3.1
PHYSICAL/MAGICAL DEF	46.2/31.7
PHYSICAL/MAGICAL ACC	28/8.8
PHYSICAL/MAGICAL EVD	7.9/2.7

EARTH	2.9	WATER	2.9	FIRE	2.9
WOOD	2.9	THUNDER	2.9	DARKNESS	2.9

SKILLS	Suvi Lei

DATA DRAIN ITEMS
Axe Bomber, Electric Guard

HELL HOUND

Species: Hound

LEVEL	29	SIZE	M	DATA DRAIN MONSTER	Pup

HP/SP/PP	1210/585/890	MIND/BODY RESISTANCE	9.7/30

PHYSICAL/MAGICAL ATK	19.9/15
PHYSICAL/MAGICAL DEF	51.3/35.3
PHYSICAL/MAGICAL ACC	31/9.7
PHYSICAL/MAGICAL EVD	8.8/3.0

EARTH	2.9	WATER	0.0	FIRE	2.9
WOOD	2.9	THUNDER	2.9	DARKNESS	2.9

SKILLS	GiVak Kruz

DATA DRAIN ITEMS
Amazon Spear, Sakabatou

TETRA ARMOR

Species: Warrior (M)

LEVEL	30	SIZE	M	DATA DRAIN MONSTER	Rajin

HP/SP/PP	1250/605/920	MIND/BODY RESISTANCE	10/37

PHYSICAL/MAGICAL ATK	20.5/3.5
PHYSICAL/MAGICAL DEF	53/36.5
PHYSICAL/MAGICAL ACC	32/10
PHYSICAL/MAGICAL EVD	9.1/3.1

EARTH	3.0	WATER	3.0	FIRE	3.0
WOOD	3.0	THUNDER	15.5	DARKNESS	0.0

SKILLS	Iron Ball (x3)

DATA DRAIN ITEMS
Dante's Blades, Scarlet Autumn

PHOENIX QUEEN

Species: Bird

LEVEL	30	SIZE	M	DATA DRAIN MONSTER	Piyoko-San

HP/SP/PP	1250/605/920	MIND/BODY RESISTANCE	10/31

PHYSICAL/MAGICAL ATK	20.5/3.5
PHYSICAL/MAGICAL DEF	53/36.5
PHYSICAL/MAGICAL ACC	32/10
PHYSICAL/MAGICAL EVD	90/3.1

EARTH	0.0	WATER	3.0	FIRE	3.0
WOOD	15.2	THUNDER	3.0	DARKNESS	3.0

SKILLS	Talon (x5), RaJuk Rom

DATA DRAIN ITEMS
Devil's Axe, Dark History

MYSTERY ROCK

Species: Earth Elemental

LEVEL	30	SIZE	M	DATA DRAIN MONSTER	Moai

HP/SP/PP	1250/605/920	MIND/BODY RESISTANCE	10/61

PHYSICAL/MAGICAL ATK	20.5/3.5
PHYSICAL/MAGICAL DEF	75/36.5
PHYSICAL/MAGICAL ACC	26/10
PHYSICAL/MAGICAL EVD	9.1/3.1

EARTH	15.2	WATER	3.0	FIRE	3.0
WOOD	3.0	THUNDER	3.0	DARKNESS	3.0

SKILLS	Ap Vorma

DATA DRAIN ITEMS
Devil's Axe, Phoenix's Wing

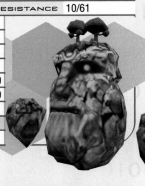

0100101010011001001001001100

DRAINED MONSTERS

This section provides all the necessary information on the creatures that the larger monsters become after being successfully Data Drained. These creatures can all be killed with a single slash of a blade, provided you can catch them. Drained monsters can't be Data Drained, nor do they yield items or Treasures upon being killed.

POROLIN — Species: Warrior (F)

LEVEL 0	SIZE S		
HP/SP 50/5		MIND/BODY RESISTANCE	1/1
PHYSICAL/MAGICAL ATK	2.5/0.5		
PHYSICAL/MAGICAL DEF	2.0/0.5		
PHYSICAL/MAGICAL ACC	2.0/1.0		
PHYSICAL/MAGICAL EVD	10/0.1		
EARTH 0.0	WATER 0.0	FIRE	0.0
WOOD 0.2	THUNDER 0.0	DARKNESS	0.0

FLAMER — Species: Magic-User (F)

LEVEL 0	SIZE S		
HP/SP 50/5		MIND/BODY RESISTANCE	1/1
PHYSICAL/MAGICAL ATK	0.5/1.0		
PHYSICAL/MAGICAL DEF	1.0/15		
PHYSICAL/MAGICAL ACC	1.0/2.0		
PHYSICAL/MAGICAL EVD	10/30		
EARTH 0.0	WATER 0.0	FIRE	0.0
WOOD 0.0	THUNDER 0.0	DARKNESS	0.0

PIPPY — Species: Bird

LEVEL 0	SIZE S		
HP/SP 50/5		MIND/BODY RESISTANCE	1/1
PHYSICAL/MAGICAL ATK	2.5/0.5		
PHYSICAL/MAGICAL DEF	2.0/0.5		
PHYSICAL/MAGICAL ACC	2.0/1.0		
PHYSICAL/MAGICAL EVD	10/0.1		
EARTH 0.0	WATER 0.0	FIRE	0.0
WOOD 0.2	THUNDER 0.0	DARKNESS	0.0

BAT — Species: Demon

LEVEL 0	SIZE S		
HP/SP 50/5		MIND/BODY RESISTANCE	1/1
PHYSICAL/MAGICAL ATK	2.5/1.0		
PHYSICAL/MAGICAL DEF	2.0/15		
PHYSICAL/MAGICAL ACC	2.0/2.0		
PHYSICAL/MAGICAL EVD	10/30		
EARTH 0.0	WATER 0.0	FIRE	0.0
WOOD 0.0	THUNDER 0.0	DARKNESS	0.2

MINNOW — Species: Fish

LEVEL 0	SIZE S		
HP/SP 50/5		MIND/BODY RESISTANCE	1/1
PHYSICAL/MAGICAL ATK	2.5/0.5		
PHYSICAL/MAGICAL DEF	2.0/0.5		
PHYSICAL/MAGICAL ACC	2.0/1.0		
PHYSICAL/MAGICAL EVD	10/0.1		
EARTH 0.0	WATER 0.2	FIRE	0.0
WOOD 0.0	THUNDER 0.0	DARKNESS	0.0

RAZINE — Species: Warrior (M)

LEVEL 0	SIZE S		
HP/SP 50/5		MIND/BODY RESISTANCE	1/1
PHYSICAL/MAGICAL ATK	2.5/0.5		
PHYSICAL/MAGICAL DEF	2.0/0.5		
PHYSICAL/MAGICAL ACC	2.0/1.0		
PHYSICAL/MAGICAL EVD	10/0.1		
EARTH 0.0	WATER 0.0	FIRE	0.0
WOOD 0.0	THUNDER 0.5	DARKNESS	0.0

LONG LIVED — Species: Magic-User (M)

LEVEL 0	SIZE S		
HP/SP 50/5		MIND/BODY RESISTANCE	1/1
PHYSICAL/MAGICAL ATK	0.5/1.0		
PHYSICAL/MAGICAL DEF	1.0/15		
PHYSICAL/MAGICAL ACC	1.0/2.0		
PHYSICAL/MAGICAL EVD	10/30		
EARTH 0.0	WATER 0.0	FIRE	0.0
WOOD 0.0	THUNDER 0.0	DARKNESS	0.0

KAKASINGER — Species: Golem

LEVEL 0	SIZE S		
HP/SP 50/5		MIND/BODY RESISTANCE	100/100
PHYSICAL/MAGICAL ATK	2.5/0.5		
PHYSICAL/MAGICAL DEF	15/0.5		
PHYSICAL/MAGICAL ACC	2.0/1.0		
PHYSICAL/MAGICAL EVD	10/0.1		
EARTH 0.2	WATER 0.0	FIRE	0.0
WOOD 0.0	THUNDER 0.0	DARKNESS	0.0

MONKEY CRAB — Species: Crustacean

LEVEL 0	SIZE S		
HP/SP 50/5		MIND/BODY RESISTANCE	1/1
PHYSICAL/MAGICAL ATK	2.5/0.5		
PHYSICAL/MAGICAL DEF	15/0.5		
PHYSICAL/MAGICAL ACC	2.0/1.0		
PHYSICAL/MAGICAL EVD	10/0.1		
EARTH 0.0	WATER 0.0	FIRE	0.0
WOOD 0.0	THUNDER 0.0	DARKNESS	0.0

MOAI — Species: Earth Elemental

LEVEL 0	SIZE S		
HP/SP 50/5		MIND/BODY RESISTANCE	1/1
PHYSICAL/MAGICAL ATK	2.5/0.5		
PHYSICAL/MAGICAL DEF	15/0.5		
PHYSICAL/MAGICAL ACC	2.0/1.0		
PHYSICAL/MAGICAL EVD	10/0.1		
EARTH 0.2	WATER 0.0	FIRE	0.0
WOOD 0.0	THUNDER 0.0	DARKNESS	0.0

GREMLIN — Species: Goblin

LEVEL 0	SIZE S		
HP/SP 50/5		MIND/BODY RESISTANCE	1/1
PHYSICAL/MAGICAL ATK	2.5/0.5		
PHYSICAL/MAGICAL DEF	2.0/0.5		
PHYSICAL/MAGICAL ACC	2.0/1.0		
PHYSICAL/MAGICAL EVD	10/0.1		
EARTH 0.2	WATER 0.0	FIRE	0.0
WOOD 0.0	THUNDER 0.0	DARKNESS	0.0

LITTLE DOGGIE
Species: Hound

LEVEL	0	SIZE	S		
HP/SP	50/5		MIND/BODY RESISTANCE	1/1	
PHYSICAL/MAGICAL ATK		2.5/0.5			
PHYSICAL/MAGICAL DEF		2.0/0.5			
PHYSICAL/MAGICAL ACC		2.0/1.0			
PHYSICAL/MAGICAL EVD		10/0.1			
EARTH	0.0	WATER	0.0	FIRE	0.2
WOOD	0.0	THUNDER	0.0	DARKNESS	0.0

WIGGLE SNAKE
Species: Statue

LEVEL	0	SIZE	S		
HP/SP	50/5		MIND/BODY RESISTANCE	100/100	
PHYSICAL/MAGICAL ATK		2.5/1.0			
PHYSICAL/MAGICAL DEF		2.0/0.5			
PHYSICAL/MAGICAL ACC		2.0/2.0			
PHYSICAL/MAGICAL EVD		10/30			
EARTH	0.0	WATER	0.0	FIRE	0.0
WOOD	0.0	THUNDER	0.2	DARKNESS	0.0

LIMP KNIFE
Species: Knife

LEVEL	0	SIZE	S		
HP/SP	50/5		MIND/BODY RESISTANCE	4/4	
PHYSICAL/MAGICAL ATK		2.5/0.5			
PHYSICAL/MAGICAL DEF		2.0/0.5			
PHYSICAL/MAGICAL ACC		2.0/1.0			
PHYSICAL/MAGICAL EVD		10/0.1			
EARTH	0.0	WATER	0.0	FIRE	0.0
WOOD	0.0	THUNDER	0.0	DARKNESS	0.0

DRAGON PUPPY
Species: Lizard

LEVEL	0	SIZE	S		
HP/SP	50/5		MIND/BODY RESISTANCE	1/1	
PHYSICAL/MAGICAL ATK		2.5/1.0			
PHYSICAL/MAGICAL DEF		2.0/0.5			
PHYSICAL/MAGICAL ACC		2.0/2.0			
PHYSICAL/MAGICAL EVD		10/0.1			
EARTH	0.0	WATER	0.0	FIRE	0.0
WOOD	0.0	THUNDER	0.0	DARKNESS	0.0

TWINKLE GRASS
Species: Plant

LEVEL	0	SIZE	S		
HP/SP	50/5		MIND/BODY RESISTANCE	1/1	
PHYSICAL/MAGICAL ATK		2.5/0.5			
PHYSICAL/MAGICAL DEF		2.0/0.5			
PHYSICAL/MAGICAL ACC		2.0/1.0			
PHYSICAL/MAGICAL EVD		10/0.1			
EARTH	0.0	WATER	0.0	FIRE	0.0
WOOD	0.2	THUNDER	0.0	DARKNESS	0.0

CHARMER
Species: Snake

LEVEL	0	SIZE	S		
HP/SP	50/5		MIND/BODY RESISTANCE	1/1	
PHYSICAL/MAGICAL ATK		2.5/1.0			
PHYSICAL/MAGICAL DEF		2.0/15			
PHYSICAL/MAGICAL ACC		2.0/2.0			
PHYSICAL/MAGICAL EVD		10/30			
EARTH	0.2	WATER	0.0	FIRE	0.0
WOOD	0.0	THUNDER	0.0	DARKNESS	0.0

FAKE MONEY
Species: Mimic

LEVEL	0	SIZE	S		
HP/SP	50/5		MIND/BODY RESISTANCE	100/100	
PHYSICAL/MAGICAL ATK		2.5/0.5			
PHYSICAL/MAGICAL DEF		15/1.0			
PHYSICAL/MAGICAL ACC		2.0/1.0			
PHYSICAL/MAGICAL EVD		10/30			
EARTH	0.0	WATER	0.0	FIRE	0.0
WOOD	0.0	THUNDER	0.0	DARKNESS	0.0

DEATH HEAD
Species: Undead

LEVEL	0	SIZE	S		
HP/SP	50/5		MIND/BODY RESISTANCE	1/1	
PHYSICAL/MAGICAL ATK		2.5/2.5			
PHYSICAL/MAGICAL DEF		2.0/1.0			
PHYSICAL/MAGICAL ACC		2.0/2.0			
PHYSICAL/MAGICAL EVD		10/0.1			
EARTH	0.0	WATER	0.0	FIRE	0.0
WOOD	0.0	THUNDER	0.0	DARKNESS	0.2

WIGGLY
Species: Insect

LEVEL	0	SIZE	S		
HP/SP	50/5		MIND/BODY RESISTANCE	1/1	
PHYSICAL/MAGICAL ATK		2.5/1.5			
PHYSICAL/MAGICAL DEF		2.0/0.5			
PHYSICAL/MAGICAL ACC		2.0/2.0			
PHYSICAL/MAGICAL EVD		10/0.1			
EARTH	0.0	WATER	0.0	FIRE	0.0
WOOD	0.0	THUNDER	0.0	DARKNESS	0.0

ODORO
Species: Wraith

LEVEL	0	SIZE	S		
HP/SP	50/5		MIND/BODY RESISTANCE	1/1	
PHYSICAL/MAGICAL ATK		2.5/1.0			
PHYSICAL/MAGICAL DEF		15/1.0			
PHYSICAL/MAGICAL ACC		2.0/2.0			
PHYSICAL/MAGICAL EVD		10/20			
EARTH	0.0	WATER	0.0	FIRE	0.0
WOOD	0.0	THUNDER	0.0	DARKNESS	0.0

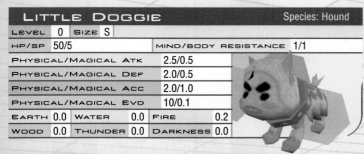

Event Characters

The sections that follow contain listings of each of the Goblins and bosses in this volume of *.hack*. These creatures are encountered through specific situations, such as an invite from the Board or via a boss fight deep in one of the dungeons.

GOBLINS

STEHONEY
Species: Goblin

LEVEL 5	SIZE S	DATA DRAIN MONSTER	N/A
HP/SP/PP 190/55/N/A		MIND/BODY RESISTANCE	20/100

PHYSICAL/MAGICAL ATK	5.5/1.0
PHYSICAL/MAGICAL DEF	10.5/26.5
PHYSICAL/MAGICAL ACC	6.0/2.5
PHYSICAL/MAGICAL EVD	1.6/99

EARTH 2.7	WATER 0.5	FIRE 0.5
WOOD 0.5	THUNDER 0.5	DARKNESS 0.5

SKILLS N/A

DATA DRAIN ITEMS

N/A

JONUE
Species: Goblin

LEVEL 10	SIZE S	DATA DRAIN MONSTER	N/A
HP/SP/PP 330/105/N/A		MIND/BODY RESISTANCE	100/30

PHYSICAL/MAGICAL ATK	8.5/1.5
PHYSICAL/MAGICAL DEF	19/38
PHYSICAL/MAGICAL ACC	10/4
PHYSICAL/MAGICAL EVD	13.1/99

EARTH 5.2	WATER 1.0	FIRE 1.0
WOOD 1.0	THUNDER 1.0	DARKNESS 1.0

SKILLS N/A

DATA DRAIN ITEMS

N/A

ZYAN
Species: Goblin

LEVEL 15	SIZE S	DATA DRAIN MONSTER	N/A
HP/SP/PP 470/155/N/A		MIND/BODY RESISTANCE	100/100

PHYSICAL/MAGICAL ATK	11.5/2.0
PHYSICAL/MAGICAL DEF	27.5/49.5
PHYSICAL/MAGICAL ACC	14/5.5
PHYSICAL/MAGICAL EVD	4.6/999

EARTH 7.7	WATER 1.5	FIRE 1.5
WOOD 1.5	THUNDER 1.5	DARKNESS 1.5

SKILLS N/A

DATA DRAIN ITEMS

N/A

ALBERT
Species: Goblin

LEVEL 25	SIZE S	DATA DRAIN MONSTER	N/A
HP/SP/PP 750/255/N/A		MIND/BODY RESISTANCE	0/100

PHYSICAL/MAGICAL ATK	17.5/3.0
PHYSICAL/MAGICAL DEF	95/999
PHYSICAL/MAGICAL ACC	22/8.5
PHYSICAL/MAGICAL EVD	67.5/999

EARTH 12.7	WATER 2.5	FIRE 2.5
WOOD 2.5	THUNDER 2.5	DARKNESS 2.5

SKILLS N/A

DATA DRAIN ITEMS

N/A

MARTINA
Species: Goblin

LEVEL 30	SIZE S	DATA DRAIN MONSTER	N/A
HP/SP/PP 890/305/N/A		MIND/BODY RESISTANCE	100/100

PHYSICAL/MAGICAL ATK	20.5/7.0
PHYSICAL/MAGICAL DEF	85/999
PHYSICAL/MAGICAL ACC	26/26
PHYSICAL/MAGICAL EVD	79/999

EARTH 99	WATER 99	FIRE 99
WOOD 99	THUNDER 99	DARKNESS 99

SKILLS Rig Saem, Dek Do

DATA DRAIN ITEMS

N/A

RAISING
A GRUNTY

ADDITIONAL
ELEMENTS

TRADE
LIST

BOOKS
OF RYU

BESTIARY

BOSSES

HE*DHUNTER

				Species: Undead
LEVEL	5	DATA DRAIN BOSS		Headhunter
SIZE	M	DATA DRAIN MONSTER		Fophead
HP/SP/PP	20,065/55/625	MIND/BODY RESISTANCE		100/100

PHYSICAL/MAGICAL ATK	6.5/1.0
PHYSICAL/MAGICAL DEF	10.5/7.0
PHYSICAL/MAGICAL ACC	7.0/2.5
PHYSICAL/MAGICAL EVD	1.6/0.6

EARTH	0.5	WATER	0.5	FIRE	0.5
WOOD	0.5	THUNDER	0.0	DARKNESS	2.7

SKILLS	Ani Zot

DATA DRAIN ITEMS
Virus Core C

*ED %YR#

				Species: Lizard
LEVEL	8	DATA DRAIN BOSS		Red Wyrm
SIZE	L	DATA DRAIN MONSTER		Dragon Puppy
HP/SP/PP	20,104/85/1250	MIND/BODY RESISTANCE		100/100

PHYSICAL/MAGICAL ATK	8.9/2.6
PHYSICAL/MAGICAL DEF	15.6/10.1
PHYSICAL/MAGICAL ACC	10/8.4
PHYSICAL/MAGICAL EVD	2.5/2.5

EARTH	0.8	WATER	0.8	FIRE	0.8
WOOD	0.8	THUNDER	0.8	DARKNESS	0.8

SKILLS	Breath, Vak Kruz

DATA DRAIN ITEMS
Virus Core M

*#TONE %URTL

				Species: Earth Elemental
LEVEL	13	DATA DRAIN BOSS		Stone Turtle
SIZE	L	DATA DRAIN MONSTER		Moai
HP/SP/PP	20,169/1090/2000	MIND/BODY RESISTANCE		100/100

PHYSICAL/MAGICAL ATK	12.9/7.5
PHYSICAL/MAGICAL DEF	41/16.1
PHYSICAL/MAGICAL ACC	12.4/4.9
PHYSICAL/MAGICAL EVD	4.0/1.4

EARTH	6.7	WATER	1.3	FIRE	1.3
WOOD	0.0	THUNDER	1.3	DARKNESS	1.3

SKILLS	GiGan Don

DATA DRAIN ITEMS
Virus Core N

K$LLER SN⊛K*R

				Species: Snake
LEVEL	16	DATA DRAIN BOSS		Killer Snaker
SIZE	L	DATA DRAIN MONSTER		Snakecharmer
HP/SP/PP	20,208/165/2450	MIND/BODY RESISTANCE		100/100

PHYSICAL/MAGICAL ATK	15.3/9.0
PHYSICAL/MAGICAL DEF	29.2/34.2
PHYSICAL/MAGICAL ACC	18.0/14.8
PHYSICAL/MAGICAL EVD	4.9/62

EARTH	8.2	WATER	1.6	FIRE	1.6
WOOD	0.0	THUNDER	1.6	DARKNESS	1.6

SKILLS	MeGan Rom

DATA DRAIN ITEMS
Virus Core P

W#ODST%CK

				Species: Plant
LEVEL	18	DATA DRAIN BOSS		Woodstock
SIZE	L	DATA DRAIN MONSTER		Sunnyflower
HP/SP/PP	20,234/185/2750	MIND/BODY RESISTANCE		100/100

PHYSICAL/MAGICAL ATK	16.9/9.5
PHYSICAL/MAGICAL DEF	32.6/22.1
PHYSICAL/MAGICAL ACC	20/6.4
PHYSICAL/MAGICAL EVD	5.5/1.9

EARTH	0.0	WATER	1.8	FIRE	1.8
WOOD	11	THUNDER	1.8	DARKNESS	1.8

SKILLS	RaJuk Rom

DATA DRAIN ITEMS
Virus Core Q

PARASITE DRAGON

				Species: Lizard
LEVEL	30	DATA DRAIN BOSS		
SIZE	L	DATA DRAIN MONSTER		Dragon Puppy
HP/SP/PP	9999/305/8888	MIND/BODY RESISTANCE		100/100

PHYSICAL/MAGICAL ATK	30/7.0
PHYSICAL/MAGICAL DEF	99/99
PHYSICAL/MAGICAL ACC	99/99
PHYSICAL/MAGICAL EVD	9.1/9.1

EARTH	20	WATER	20	FIRE	20
WOOD	20	THUNDER	20	DARKNESS	20

SKILLS	Breath (High/Low), Ranki Lei

DATA DRAIN ITEMS
Hyakkidouran

01001010100110010010010010001100

FINAL BOSSES

SKEITH			Species: N/A
LEVEL 99	SIZE N/A	DATA DRAIN MONSTER	Skeith
HP/SP/PP 30,000/999/9000		MIND/BODY RESISTANCE	100/100
PHYSICAL/MAGICAL ATK		20/20	
PHYSICAL/MAGICAL DEF		90/90	
PHYSICAL/MAGICAL ACC		99/99	
PHYSICAL/MAGICAL EVD		6.1/6.1	
EARTH 10.5	WATER 10.5	FIRE	10.5
WOOD 10.5	THUNDER 10.5	DARKNESS	10.5
SKILLS	Execution, Darkness, Judgement, Darkness (Epitaph)		
DATA DRAIN ITEMS			
Virus Core F			

SKEITH (POST-DATA DRAIN)			Species: N/A
LEVEL 00	SIZE 00	DATA DRAIN MONSTER	N/A
HP/SP/PP 4500/999/N/A		MIND/BODY RESISTANCE	100/100
PHYSICAL/MAGICAL ATK		20/20	
PHYSICAL/MAGICAL DEF		90/90	
PHYSICAL/MAGICAL ACC		99/99	
PHYSICAL/MAGICAL EVD		6.1/6.1	
EARTH 10.5	WATER 10.5	FIRE	10.5
WOOD 10.5	THUNDER 10.5	DARKNESS	10.5
SKILLS	Darkness		
DATA DRAIN ITEMS			
N/A			

Monster-Only Skills

The vast majority of the skills used by the monsters in battle are identical to the ones Kite and his friends have at their disposal. Nevertheless, there are a few special skills that only a select number of monsters can utilize. These skills are listed in the following table.

PHYSICAL ATTACK SKILLS

NAME	SKILL	ELEMENT	TARGET	ATK	ACC	SP
General Armor	Iron Ball (x3)	N/A	Unit	2	0	0
Metal Emperor	Triple Crush	N/A	Unit	5	15	0
Scorpion Tank	Tail	N/A	Unit	5	50	0
Iron Ball Freak	Two-Hand Bash	Darkness	Unit	5	5	0
Flameheads	Breath (x4)	Fire	Group	10	3	0
Sword of Chaos	Spin Slash (x3)	N/A	Group	1	5	0
Dust Curse	Spin Slash (x3)	N/A	Group	1	5	0
Armor Shogun	Wild Shot (x11)	Fire	Unit	1	5	0
Lead Snakoid	Two-Hand Slash (x7)	N/A	Group	5	15	0
Red Wyrm	Breath	Fire	Group	5	50	0
Lamia Fighter	Bite (x5)	N/A	Unit	1	5	0

MAGICAL ATTACK SKILLS

NAME	SKILL	LEVEL	ELEMENT	TARGET	ATK	ACC	SP
Dark Rider	BiAni Don	2	Darkness	Group	8	20	20

OFFICIAL STRATEGY GUIDE

An Imprint of Pearson Education
201 West 103rd Street
Indianapolis, Indiana 46290

ISBN: 0-7440-0204-4

Library of Congress Catalog No.: 2003100284

Printing Code: The rightmost double-digit number is the year of the book's printing; the rightmost single-digit number is the number of the book's printing. For example, 03-1 shows that the first printing of the book occurred in 2003.

06   05   04   03   4   3   2   1

Manufactured in the United States of America.

BRADYGAMES STAFF

Publisher
David Waybright

Editor-In-Chief
H. Leigh Davis

Creative Director
Robin Lasek

Marketing Manager
Janet Eshenour

Licensing Manager
Mike Degler

Assistant Marketing Manager
Susie Nieman

CREDITS

Title Manager
Tim Cox

Screenshot Editor
Michael Owen

Book Designer
Ann-Marie Deets

Production Designer
Bob Klunder

ACKNOWLEDGMENTS

This book would not have been possible without the patience and support provided by my editor, Tim Cox. It was a long time coming but my first RPG project is now behind me, thank you for smoothing out the bumps in the road! I'd like to also thank BradyGames' Leigh Davis for the opportunity to work on such a unique project. I'd also like to thank Mike Degler of BradyGames and Linda Shannon and Minako Takahashi of Bandai for seeing that all of my questions were answered. Special thanks to Doug Dlin for his excellent translation skills. Last, but not least, I'd like to acknowledge my lovely wife Kristin for helping compile the data for the many appendices in this book—I couldn't have done it without you!

DEDICATION

This book is dedicated to my mother, who has hit every snag and obstacle life can possibly throw her way, and still manages to make her children proud. The nest might finally be empty, but you're not forgotten.

COMING SOON!

悪性変異

DOT **.hack**™ Part 2
M U T A T I O N

AND

THE

STORY

CONTINUES...

www.dothack.com
Sadamoto • Ito • Mashimo

 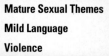